P9-DII-241

WHAT
DEMONS
CAN DO
TO SAINTS

WHAT DEMONS CAN DO TO SAINTS

Merrill F. Unger

MOODY PRESS
CHICAGO

© 1991 by
THE MOODY BIBLE INSTITUTE
OF CHICAGO

Originally published in 1977

All rights reserved. No part of this book may be reproduced in any form without permission in writing from the publisher, except in the case of brief quotations embodied in critical articles or reviews.

All Scripture quotations, unless noted otherwise, are from the King James Version. Quotations from the *New American Standard Bible,* © 1960, 1962, 1963, 1968, 1971, 1972, 1973, 1975, and 1977 by The Lockman Foundation, are used by permission.

ISBN: 0-8024-9418-8

7 9 10 8 6

Printed in the United States of America

CONTENTS

92003

FOREWORD

A nd by faith He still speaks, even though He is dead" (He-brews 11:4*b*; NIV). These inspired words concerning Abel have appropriate application to Merrill F. Unger. All of chris-tendom has benefited from the scholarly pen of Merrill Unger. Evangelical Christians have gladly owned him as one of their most able spokesmen for the Christian faith. He is the author of some twenty-seven books and many published arti-cles. His contribution of scholarly assistance in numerous fields of biblical study is almost legendary. Most pastors, mis-sionaries, and Christian workers of various disciplines have several volumes of Dr. Unger's reference books in their librar-ies. His prodigious work still bears much fruit for the cause of Christ.

During his writing years, Dr. Unger devoted concentrat-ed study toward understanding a biblical view of demono-logy. In 1965, he authored a well received book on the topic of this neglected subject entitled *Biblical Demonology* (Scrip-ture Press, 1965). His vital interest in the subject continued to develop as he authored such subsequent studies as *Demons in the World Today* (Tyndale, 1971) and *The Haunting of Bishop Pike* (Tyndale, 1971). His last work on this special interest subject was published in 1977 under the title *What Demons Can Do to Saints* (Moody, 1977).

Dr. Unger died in 1980, three years after this last book on demonology was published. As he came toward the close of his earthly life, the Holy Spirit seemed to be sharing with Merrill Unger an urgent message of warning for believers. He writes, "Saints must realize that they are the bull's eye, as it were, against which Satan and his demonic helpers aim their fiery darts." Dr. Unger did not live to see how urgently needed his warning message would be. A blast of Satanic activity was in the making. The opening of America during the '80s to a variety of occultic interests and the widespread ritualistic worship of Satan came upon our culture like a plague.

Unprecedented numbers of people became involved in this occultic search, triggering serious demonic problems in the lives of those who dabble in such things. The alarm has finally sounded in nearly every expression of Christ's church. We are seeing that we really are involved in a deadly war with the powers of darkness. Churches must be ready to minister to those affected. Some of those desperately needing help have grown up in our churches. Drug experimentation, promiscuity, heavy metal music, and dabbling in Satanism has touched the young people of many Christian homes. Breaking away from involvement in such deceptions of darkness sometimes comes hard. Biblical help is desperately needed.

The republishing of Merrill Unger's book on *What Demons Can Do to Saints* provides an important assistance toward supplying biblical help. He deals objectively and with sensitivity concerning the degree of demonization Christians might experience. Although not everyone may agree with his conclusions, everyone should consider his careful approach to the subject. His warnings about seeking for "a physical and emotional experience not authenticated by the Word of God" are well documented by illustrations from the lives of those who came into bondage by such seeking. His chapter on "Mediumship in Pious Masquerade" is of classic importance for protection from the New Age deceptions that are bursting upon the church. Although his treatment of gaining freedom from demonic troubling is limited, his observations are necessary and helpful.

Many of us who desire to maintain biblical balance in this day of extremes greatly welcome this return of Dr. Unger's book to print. I prayerfully trust that it will receive the wide audience of readers that it deserves.

MARK I. BUBECK

PREFACE TO ORIGINAL EDITION

Another book on Satan and demons? The market is glutted with literature on the subject, and there is an almost fanatical preoccupation with the supernatural and the occult manifest in many quarters. One might well wonder at the wisdom of adding another title to an already lengthy list.

But this is not just "another book" on the subject. It is the answer to a perplexing and ever-pressing problem. Wherever I go, people ask one question more than any other, "Can a Christian be indwelt by a demon? Can a child of God be demon possessed?"

The uncertainty and confusion that exists in the minds of many of the Lord's people on this subject is amazing. Convictions range from one extreme to the other.

Many Christians believe that the powers of darkness can do practically nothing to a truly regenerated person. Others believe that they can do practically everything to them, including dragging them to perdition.

What does the Word of God say? How far can Satan and demons go in the life of a seriously sinning saint? What is the ultimate to which the powers of darkness can go when the child of God pulls out all the stops to sin?

A study of this important theme is long overdue. May God use this exposition of what the Word of God says on the subject to bless and stabilize His people in a time of unparalleled spiritual peril.

1

PRIME TARGET OF THE DEVIL

In an age of accelerated activity of the powers of darkness, the question of the moment is how far Satan and demons can go in working havoc in the people of God. The answer to this problem is pressing in its urgency because of widespread ignorance and uncertainty that exist on the subject among God's people. The rapid spread of occultism in our times has, to some extent, dissipated disbelief in the reality and inworking of demonic forces in the lives of the unregenerate. People who once viewed Satan and evil spirits as figments of the imagination or, at best, hangovers from medieval superstition, are more inclined today to believe in a real devil and demons. These sinister beings are held not only to influence people but actually to indwell them and upon occasion to be exorcized from them.

But strangely enough, while many unsaved people sense the reality and power of the realm of evil supernaturalism, many Christians remain skeptical and naive. Usually believers readily grant the wide range of demonic operation in the unsaved. Yet, often the concept of the extent of satanic and demonic activity in the life of a believer is circumscribed and inadequate. It tends to be theological and theoretical rather than biblical and practical.

The nature of the times in which we live calls for clarification of the precise role Satan and demons may play in the life and experience of a believer. This in turn necessitates a study of the career of Satan and his kingdom of demon helpers. The purpose is to show why these powers of darkness are arrayed against man, particularly against regenerate man.

FACING A FEARFUL FOE

Although there are many things about Satan and demonic powers that revealed truth does not tell us, one thing is transparently clear. In these sinister spirit personalities, humanity, especially redeemed humanity, has an implacable enemy. This foe is dedicated to alienate man from God and to keep him from Christ's saving grace. When men do believe the gospel, Satan exerts every effort to turn them away from God's will. He knows that once they are saved they are beyond his power insofar as their position before God and their eternal destiny are concerned. So he determines to do them as much damage as he can, seeking to ruin their Christian life and testimony for God.

Satan is relentless and pitiless in his hatred for God and the people of God. What makes the devil a fearful foe is the fact of his great power. This is augmented by the assistance of innumerable fallen angels or demons. Consequently, satanic forces constitute a mighty, evil spiritual reality to be seriously reckoned with by the entire fallen race, both redeemed and unredeemed.

Actually Satan is the most powerful person in the universe after God.[1] Although he is a creature and a vast gap separates him as such from the Creator, he is the first creature and evidently the most glorious of all creatures. Even though he fell and his glory was corrupted by sin, he is still correctly styled as "his infernal majesty." Dave Breese discusses Satan's ten most believable lies under this apt designation.[2]

Our Lord plainly intimated that Satan is a king and presides over a kingdom (Matthew 12:26). As a potentate reigning over the realm of spiritual darkness, Satan extends his sway over the evil angels or demons. Through these "principalities, powers, rulers of the darkness of this world and wicked spirits in the heavenlies" (Ephesians 6:12), he exerts dominion over the fallen human race. As men open the door to him by sin and rebellion against God, he enters to dominate and enslave.

WHY SATAN AND DEMONS OPPOSE MEN

The malignity of Satan and his hosts against mankind reaches back to the creation of Lucifer and the angels in dim antiquity. According to intimations given through the prophets Isaiah (14:12-14) and Ezekiel (28:11-19), Satan fell from his original sinless state. When he rebelled against the Creator, Satan drew with him a great number of his angelic colleagues. These apparently became the fallen angels or demons (cf. Revelation 12:7-9).

Satan's fall and the entrance of sin into a hitherto sinless universe presented a grave problem. How would the infinitely holy and loving Creator deal with sin and rebellion in His angelic creatures? Would He allow them to go on forever as free and unimprisoned rebels to roam His universe? Or would He institute a plan to bring an end to sin by rigidly isolating sinners?

It was this latter plan of eventually isolating sin and sinners that God had in mind from all eternity. To accomplish it He created man upon the earth. This planet was selected to be man's abode, evidently because sin began here in connection with the fall of Satan and the angels (Genesis 1:2; cf. Job 38:5-7). Here, where sin arose, God would show how He, in His infinite love and holiness, would deal with it and put it down forever.

To this end God created man innocent, but with the power of free choice to obey or disobey his Creator. Satan's malignant subtlety was directed against man because the evil one desired to frustrate the divine plan and enslave the human race. This he accomplished, at least to a degree, by the temptation and fall of man.

But Satan did not fully reckon on God's gracious program of redemption in Christ. He failed to count on its final outcome in effecting his own undoing and that of the rebel angels and wicked men who would follow him (Matthew 25:41; Revelation 20:11-15).

Satan in Scripture revelation is presented as irremediably confirmed in rebellion against God. He is also portrayed as unchangeably dedicated to doing as much damage as possible to mankind, especially the redeemed. His attack upon the saints is relentless and implacable. He opposes them as he opposed Christ when Christ was upon the earth. The saints represent his ultimate destruction, as Christ does, because they are united to Christ and share His triumph over him and his hosts (1 Corinthians 12:12; Ephesians 1:20-23; Revelation 20:1-3, 10).

The saints must realize that they are the bull's-eye, as it were, against which Satan and his demon helpers aim their most fiery darts. They constitute Satan's deadliest foes and the greatest threat to his authority and power. This is why saints dare not be oblivious of Satan's malignity nor "ignorant of his devices" (2 Corinthians 3:11).

It is high time for believers to see Satan and demonic powers in their true light and full Scripture perspective. The age of the demon or the era of the occult in which we find ourselves is no time to be naive concerning the powers of darkness. To deny the reality of Satan and demons has little appeal these days. Such a conclusion may satisfy a naturalistic theorist; however, it carries little weight with a man who gives the Scriptures credence or who honestly faces the facts of life.

On the other hand, many who hold Scripture in high esteem and respect its testimony concerning Satan and demons, in actual practice entertain a concept of these forces that is theoretical rather than scriptural and practical, especially as far as demons are concerned. Today many believers simply do not face the issue of the degree to which demonic powers can take over in their lives if they open the door to them.

There is, in fact, a strong tendency among many Christians to be naive concerning their arch foe, Satan, and his demon assistants. This is especially so in relation to the question of demonism as it may affect the saint. Such a situation is perilous, for to be ignorant or misinformed on this subject is weighted with dire risks. This becomes apparent when the Christian warrior realizes that he is the target of demonic strategy and attack.

In its spiritual conflict, the church of Christ must obviously be knowledgeable about its foes. In wars on the human plane, military strategists are keenly aware of the necessity of knowing the enemy. Accordingly, they employ intricate networks of intelligence and counterintelligence. Missions involving espionage are frequently as crucial to winning a war as actual battles. Without intelligence of the enemy's strength and position, the results of any military encounter would be highly dubious. Yet believers sometimes display an obvious disinterest in what the Bible reveals about Satan and demons. Or, what is even worse, they manifest a morbid fear of such a study. This apathy or dread is almost as perilous as the opposite extreme of fanatical occupation with evil. Such extremists ride demonism as a hobby, seeing demons in everybody and everything. Obviously these aberrations are a delight to Satan. They prove the subtlety of his stratagems by which he outwits his opponents and gains advantage over them.

The only sane approach is to know the enemy. Only as his wiles are laid bare will the believer be able to anticipate and outmaneuver him. Satan's chief tactics are to hide his identity and his assaults. The Christian must recognize him and anticipate his moves.

Only as the believer knows the powers of darkness will he be able to win against them in his superior position and strength in Christ. The rampant demon activity of these last days (1 Timothy 4:1) issues a clarion call to every friend of Christ: "Know your foe!"

WHAT THE DEVIL FEARS MOST

Although Satan's foes do not always know their enemy, one thing is sure. Satan *always* knows his foes. He is thoroughly acquainted with them and is quite aware of those who fall to his strategies and are consequently comparatively harmless. He also knows those who recognize and count on their position in Christ and who find and fulfill God's will for their lives. These saints are what the devil fears most, for they constitute the deadliest threat to his plans and ambitions.

It is against the latter group of saints that Satan launches his most subtle attacks. Protected with the full armor of God, they are endued with God's full power and have complete victory over Satan and his minions. Therefore Satan does his best to lure them away from trusting in the impregnable fortress of their position in Christ.

The evil one delights to see a saint become occupied with what he is or does in himself rather than with what he is or does in his position in Christ. This is tantamount to leaving the protection of the mighty fortress God has provided in Christ for the perils of the unprotected open field.

Exposed and unprotected in this manner, the Christian arouses little terror as far as Satan and demonic powers are concerned. And little wonder! The Christian is a pushover for evil powers when he tries to face them in his own strength. It is the omnipotent power of God that Satan dreads, and that power only becomes available to the believer as he counts on what Christ has done for him and is waiting to do through him in response to his faith.

This attitude of confidence in what he is in union with Christ expresses itself in what the believer thinks, says, and does. In this radiant atmosphere of faith in his crucified, risen, and ascended Lord, the believer's every thought, word, or deed becomes a terror to the enemy. Whether he prays, witnesses, worships, or just discharges the everyday duties of life, the believer who centers his faith in His divine Savior and what he is in Him is the one thing that causes the powers of darkness to tremble.

It is true, according to the old adage, that "the devil trembles when he sees the weakest saint upon his knees." But it is just as true that he and his cohorts tremble when they see the weakest saint in any activity of the Christian life, where he puts his faith in his all-victorious Lord, for then that saint becomes their strongest foe. The powers of darkness stand in awful fear and dread of Him who "spoiled principalities and powers" and who "made a shew of them openly, triumphing over them in it" (Colossians 2:15).

They experience that same fear and dread of any believer who will dare by faith to count on his union with his all-victorious Lord. Such a believer becomes Satan's prime target. All hell's artillery is hurled against him, because he constitutes the deadliest enemy the powers of darkness possess.

2

LOOK OUT FOR SATAN'S TRICKS!

Satan is a trickster, a deceiver, a dangerous prevaricator. Although he manifests his deception toward all mankind, he directs his cleverest tricks and most wily deception against redeemed humanity. The more spiritual and victorious the believer, the more subtle and vehement are the satanic and demonic assaults against him.

Scripture calls these cunning artifices "wiles." "Put on the whole armour of God, that ye may be able to stand against the *wiles* of the devil" (Ephesians 6: 11; italics added*). The Greek word is *methodia*, from which we get our word "method," usually with a good connotation. But as used of Satan, the word is evil in its meaning and denotes "a deceitful scheme" or "treacherous artifice."

Satan is full of deceptive tricks because his whole purpose is to delude the believer. Having failed to keep him in blindness and unbelief concerning the gospel of God's grace, he tries the next best ruse by employing every strategy his perverted wisdom can conjure up to divert the believer from God's Word and will.

As a fisherman uses a lure to draw a fish to a hidden hook and as a hunter conceals a trap for the unwary animal, Satan lays his snares for God's child. His ultimate purpose is

---

* In future Scripture quotations, all italics have been added for the sake of emphasis and will not be noted.

to divert worship and service away from God toward himself. Failing this, he resorts to every conceivable device to cripple a believer's effectiveness in witness and service for God. He does not stop until he and his demon helpers have either utterly despoiled the believer or else cut short his physical life by premature death (1 John 5:16).

TRICK 1: "WORSHIP ME, NOT GOD!"

Satan's oldest and "most deadly game" is to divert man's worship from God, directing it instead toward other "gods" and ultimately toward himself. This crafty device is the expression of Satan's original and all-consuming passion to make himself "like the Most High" (Isaiah 14:14; NASB*). This basic motive of blasphemous self-exaltation is revealed in the record of his first sin, which was the beginning of sin in an originally sinless universe. It reappears three times in scriptural revelation, and "these disclosures stand out like milestones in Satan's career."[2]

When Satan confronted the first Adam in Eden, Satan was ready to foist upon Adam his own unholy ideal of proud self-promotion. "You will be like God" (Genesis 3:5; NASB). Daringly, when he confronted the last Adam, whom he well knew to be God incarnate, he manifested the same desire to usurp the place of God. His suggestion was utterly blasphemous: "If you worship . . . me" (Luke 4:7; NASB).

Satan's motive will be fully laid bare when the man of sin, the terrible Antichrist, "opposes and exalts himself above every so-called god or object of worship, so that he takes his seat in the temple of God, displaying himself as being God" (2 Thessalonians 2:4; NASB).

Satan's game of making himself like God has many subtle variations. It displays itself in the various forms of idolatry. It appears in the worship of other gods, self, the world, the flesh, or in its ultimate form, the worship of Satan himself.

---

* *New American Standard Bible*

Today satanism is a growing cult. Actual churches of Satan, openly dedicated to worshiping the devil, are springing up here and there in America and around the world. One such church in San Francisco was founded in 1967 by Anton LaVey.[3]

Satanism, moreover, is not an empty fad but, rather, a sinister spiritual reality. Satan has power, and he offers to share that power with those who will worship him. But it is an evil power, for it is a power that is apart from God and actually in opposition to God. It may offer results that on the surface appear to be good, such as physical healing, a way out from drug addiction or alcoholism, or the occult ability to effect miracles (magic) or to foretell the future.

But the apparent good is only an attractive bait to bind the victim with crueler chains and to supply a new "high" that in the end will prove a new low in the life of the Satan-shackled person.

If Satan had the immense effrontery to offer this alluring route to power and glory to the Lord of heaven, dare we presume for one moment that he will not play this nefarious game with our Lord's own here on earth?

In fact, in one form or another, Satan and his demon helpers are constantly trying to foist this trick upon believers. Through halo-crowned idolatry the devil seeks to turn Christians away from complete allegiance to God to some form of devotion to another object of worship, some other "god" under the guise of some thing or person, notably one's own self.[4]

So rampant is this peril that the apostle John warns the children of God to be ever on the alert against it. Constantly the believer must be aware of this wile of the devil. The apostle John realized how God's people are continually assaulted by Satan with this trick.[5] His somber warning rings out: "Little children, guard yourselves from idols" (1 John 5:21; NASB).

TRICK 2: "I OR MY DEMONS DON'T EXIST"

The ruse of denying his existence is an exceedingly common practice of Satan. By means of this deception, he plays a subtle game of hide-and-seek and appears incognito. When his mask is in danger of being detected, he throws up a smoke screen and hides behind it. When his presence is suspected and the activity of his demons is discerned, he raises a hue and cry, "It's nothing but superstition."

In fact, the widespread departure from historical, biblical Christianity and the resulting secularization of society both in communist lands and in the Western world since World War I, created an atmosphere in which it was popular to relegate the whole concept of Satan, demons, witches, and magic to the superstitious Dark Ages.

Phenomenal advances in science and the emergence of a highly developed technological culture helped to brand belief in Satan and demons a pure fancy. Satan's subtle trick succeeded with millions. No devil, no demons, no such beings as witches and wizards, mediums or occult prognosticators were recognized as realities.

Even some Bible scholars felt they must demythologize the Bible, especially in its incisive presentation of Satan and demons. Such stories, it was concluded, were graphic pre-scientific descriptions of those whom psychologists today know as mentally ill, emotionally upset, or physically afflicted.

In the meantime, Satan has been able to work unrecognized behind this smoke screen. What he has been able to get away with in the process is truly remarkable. But with crime, violence, and immorality ever on the increase in a troubled world, one wonders—with Satan and demons voted out—who is carrying on their work.

TRICK 3: "I AND MY DEMONS ARE EVERYWHERE!"

This is a reversal strategy. By the decade of the sixties, Satan had overplayed his game of hide-and-seek. When he could no longer convince people that all belief in spirits is superstitious, a new tactic was needed. Now his game would be directed toward inculcating superstition instead of employing it as a mask to hide his identity.

Up to the dawn of the age of the occult, the so-called age of Aquarius, in the decade of the seventies, Satan had been crying, "No devil or demons anywhere!" Then he reversed himself and began popularizing the idea, "Satan and demons everywhere!"

Those who fall for the "demons, demons everywhere" strategy become addicted to the idea that demons cause almost every emotional, mental, spiritual, or physical problem. They become fanatics in satanism and demonism. They ride it as a hobbyhorse. Like any religious hobby, this becomes a lopsided and unhealthy preoccupation.

Such a danger especially faces Christians who may be credulous. Their problem is not unbelief but credulity. Satan stands ready to take advantage of their naïveté, particularly in an era when occult religion is threatening to supplant pure biblical Christianity.

Demon activity is responsible for some physical, emotional, mental, and spiritual problems, as the Bible clearly teaches. But this is not to conclude by any means that *all* such problems have a demonic origin (cf. Matthew 4:24). For example, in demon-ridden China of the nineteenth century the natives had no difficulty differentiating between mental disease and demon-possession.[6] Dr. Alfred Lechler, a German psychologist, stresses the need to distinguish between the diseased and the demonic. In this connection he shows the difference between schizophrenia, epilepsy, depression, neurosis, psychopathy, senile dementia, and the demonic.[7] Christians must exercise every precaution to avoid falling prey to Satan's two popular tricks of either seeing Satan and demons in nothing or else seeing them in everything.

TRICK 4: "LET ME TELL YOUR FUTURE!"

Satan plays the apparently innocent game of telling the future so skillfully that he completely conceals the deadly trap behind it. "What could be wrong with satisfying an almost universal desire of knowing the future?" the devil asks.

The reply, of course, is "There is nothing wrong with knowing the future as God has outlined it in His prophetic Word." Those who love God's Word should know prophecy and rejoice in the knowledge of things to come that God would have us know for our benefit. But there is everything wrong in prying into the future, which God has not revealed and, for our own welfare, does not want us to know. Such knowledge is contrary to God's Word and will, but it is the kind of knowledge that Satan and demons give. It insults God and is at cross-purposes with His will.

Although God has revealed His general plan for the future for both the saved and the unsaved, it is not normally His purpose for us to know the specifics of that plan or the details of individual lives. The Word is clear on this matter:

> Come now, you who say, "Today or tomorrow, we shall go to such and such a city, and spend a year there and engage in business and make a profit." Yet you do not know what your life will be like tomorrow. You are just a vapor that appears for a little while and then vanishes away. Instead, you ought to say, "If the Lord wills, we shall live and also do this or that" (James 4:13-15; NASB).

Yet, how many millions of unsaved people are falling into Satan's occult snare by consulting witches and mediums, clairvoyants and astrologers? Jeane Dixon and Edgar Cayce are more popular with multitudes than are the holy Scriptures.

Nor are believers exempt from this dreadful snare of the occult. Those who attend churches that hardly preach the gospel and never expound the Word become sitting ducks for the occult lure. Starved for spiritual food and hungry to know about future things, they see the false fare of the occult prognosticators as true spiritual food. Tragically, it turns out to be poison in the pot and leads to demon deception (cf. Deuteronomy 18:9-22). If not renounced, it results in demonic oppression.

Many believers in good, sound evangelical churches are also in serious trouble in this area. Practically nothing is being said in the average evangelical church today to warn against the peril of occult contamination. The reason is, in the words of one pastor, "I don't want to advertise the devil. He is doing his own advertising."

Isaiah's warning to God's people is just as relevant today as it was in his day:

> And when they say to you "Consult the mediums and the wizards who whisper and mutter," should not a people consult their God? Should they consult the dead on behalf of the living? To the law and to the testimony! If they do not speak according to this word, it is because they have no dawn [light] (Isaiah 8:19-20; NASB).

TRICK 5: "LOOK WHAT I CAN DO"

Satan, of course, is not all-powerful, as is God. But he would like to be because of his desire to be like God. However, what power he does possess—which is considerable, though severely restricted by the Creator—he uses to the full. Like a circus clown, Satan is always ready to bring out his bag of tricks to entertain in order to deceive. God has allowed him and his demons a circumscribed sphere of operation in the natural realm in which man lives. This means that, under certain conditions, the powers of darkness can take over and transcend the laws of the natural realm by the higher laws of the spiritual realm (cf. 2 Thessalonians 2:9; Revelation 13:13).

This occurs in such spiritistic phenomena as *telekinesis* (moving objects from a distance, apart from physical force), *levitation* (causing objects to float in the air or phantoms to appear out of nowhere), *apports* (moving one solid object through another solid object), *physical healing* (cures by white or black magic), *clairvoyance* (seeing what is naturally invisible), and *clairaudience* (hearing what is naturally inaudible).

To deceive his dupes, Satan makes a cheap and flashy show of these real, though pitiably restricted, powers that God allows him. The sovereign, divine purpose in even permitting this curbed display of evil supernaturalism is punitive. It is just and necessary that those who flout the Word and will of God, and thus reject His truth, should be exposed to deception to believe the devil's lie.

The life of the late Bishop James A. Pike offers a dramatic illustration. Rejecting every cardinal tenet of historical biblical Christianity, the bishop was lured into the net of the occult. After the tragic suicide of his drug-addicted son, occult powers staged such a demonstration of spiritistic phenomena in recalling the bishop's deceased son, Jim, Jr., that Pike was drawn like a magnet into spiritism to satisfy a deep longing to communicate with his son in the spirit world.[8]

The bishop himself relates his bizarre experiences with psychic phenomena. Objects were mysteriously moved (telekinesis), hair was unexplainably singed as by fire, and the thermostat turned up without human hands. The bishop tells his tale in his controversial best seller, *The Other Side,* which perhaps as much as any other factor helped launch the present age of the occult, which began in 1970.

Alleged communication with Jim, Jr., through such world-famous mediums as Ena Twigg in England and George Daisley and Arthur Ford in America sealed Pike's doom.[9] Like King Saul of old, when he consulted the spiritistic medium at

Endor and as a result met an untimely death on the battlefield of Gilboa (1 Samuel 28, 31), so Pike had a tragic end in the desert of Judea.[10]

The bishop is not the first professing Christian who has fallen to the satanic strategy of "Look what I can do." This is perhaps the devil's most popular approach in a day when occult religion is growing in power and appeal. When Christians drift away from pure, biblical Christianity, Satan's counterfeit offers a cheap but alluring substitute. If Christ's person and finished redemptive work become peripheral, some form of occult religionism will become central.

The choice is inevitable. Christ must be central, or Satan will trick the saint into putting something or somebody else in the place that only Christ should occupy. If this is done, Satan will not rest until he has deceived his victim into subscribing to his magical tricks in place of the power of God.

TRICK 6: "LOOK WHAT A NICE FELLOW I AM!"

Satan is great at wearing masks. In fact, his whole career is like a masquerade party. Evil though he is and operating as he does in the realm of darkness, he nevertheless loves to disguise himself as "an angel of light" (2 Corinthians 11:14) and "a good guy." In this role he is eminently successful and presents a special peril to the believer.

How many new converts have been trapped by a cult because the leader or followers were nice, loving, and kind? As Stan Baldwin points out, "By a true test, many very nice people in false cults and non-Christian religions, as well as many nice atheists, agnostics, and ordinary 'good-hearted' sinners, are revealed to be under Satan's control."[11]

Actually it is terrifying to contemplate the danger that faces a newly regenerated person in today's occult-ridden religious world. Almost as helpless as a newborn baby in the natural world is the newly born-again soul in the spiritual realm. New converts must immediately be given "the pure milk of the word, that by it . . . [they] may grow in respect to salvation" (1 Peter 2:2; NASB).

The tragedy is that unless the new convert is directed into a Bible-believing church and taught sound doctrine from the start, he becomes a helpless pawn on the devil's chessboard. Satan is deftly playing his shrewd game of "Look what a nice guy I am." Who can tell into what error or "doctrines of demons" (1 Timothy 4:1; NASB) the child of God, bereft of sound teaching to guide him (1 John 4:1-2), will fall in these days of abysmal religious confusion?

Scores of dangerous cults lie in wait today to catch the unwary feet of the child of God who may wander from the path of the Word of God. The demonic nature of each is basically revealed by the application of this acid test given in the Word of God: "By this you know the Spirit of God: every spirit that confesses that Jesus Christ has come in the flesh is from God; and every spirit that does not confess Jesus is not from God" (1 John 4:2-3; NASB).

This test hits the bull's-eye of all redemptive truth: the person of the God-man, Jesus Christ. Like a pebble thrown into the water, this is the central truth from which all the concentric circles of revealed truth spring, noteworthily the finished redemptive work of the Savior that is inseparably connected with His glorious person.

It is this central truth that Satan and demons attack. If it is denied or distorted, all the great truths that proceed from it are denied or distorted. And what a show Satan stages to accomplish his purpose. How subtly he puts on the saintly garb, enticingly calling spiritism "spiritualism" to deceive its dupes. How angelically he puts a halo on it by sweet double-talk, calling it "Christian spiritualism." How innocent he makes the séance appear by opening it with the Lord's Prayer, singing gospel hymns, and invoking the name of the triune God.[12] How diplomatic he is to call Jesus "The Master Medium." All this is done only to hide the real evil and conceal its demonic nature.

How craftily Satan dons his angelic disguise in astrology and occult prophecy. Edgar Cayce is presented as a true Christian. Jeane Dixon is heralded as a prophetess of the Lord. Is she not a good religious, philanthropic person? Do not she and Sybil Leek claim to use their gift only for good? Have they not made some astonishing predictions that have come true? How could this possibly not be from God?[13]

Not once do millions infatuated with the occult, ask, "What does God's Word say about this?" Nor do they stop long enough to see beyond Satan's fascinating mask of being a "nice guy."

The same is true of many notable public faith healers of the twentieth century. Insisting that physical healing is in the atonement as an immediate blessing and that, therefore, it is the divine will to heal every saint in right relation with God, they forget that God may have a definite purpose in infirmity to refine His choicest saints (2 Corinthians 12:7-10). Insisting to the contrary they fail to realize that demonic magic instead of divine miracle may come into play.

Under this "nice guy" strategy, Satan effects demonic healings that parade as the divine. Magic masquerades as miracle. Many of God's people, as a result, are deluded and despoiled. They are in a sense "healed," but there is a price tag in contrast to God's absolutely free healings.

The bill Satan sends after he has duped his victims is *always* too big for the supposed "benefit" received. Itemized, it often includes the following: faith in oneself or the healer instead of in God alone (a variety of idolatry); ensnarement in doctrinal error, some cult, or some form of imbalance or fanaticism; or, worst of all, physical "cure" but transference of the trouble to the mind or the emotions, resulting in occult bondage.

It never pays to be hoodwinked by Satan in his scheme of parading as an "angel of light" or a "good guy."

Trick 7: "God Doesn't Really Love You!"

One of Satan's oldest and most successful ruses was tried successfully on Eve. He made her doubt that God loved her. When she did that, she fell for the devil's lie and disobeyed God (Genesis 3:1-6).

Satan has been using this trick ever since. It's a bold, daring game. God's love is so real, so easy to see without hardly looking for it. Yet, that obvious fact does not stop the devil. He knows he has to brainwash any thinking person to make him blind to God's love, but he doesn't balk at this because he knows that there are always people who will listen to his line and fall for his slander.

If his victim is an unbeliever, he whispers in his ear, "Don't ever become a Christian! You will really ruin your life!" If his target is a believer, he sneers, "Don't be a fool and give your life to Christ! You *really* want to be miserable, don't you!"

If trouble comes our way, Satan is not slow to suggest that God has forgotten us or that He can't be trusted. Of course, we do not say in so many words that God does not love us. But we betray our doubts in a thousand ways by what we do and say. A Christian in a fit of self-pity cries, "Nothing ever seems to go right with me. I am a born loser!"

A believer yields his life to God. Then he is severely tested. He promptly forgets all God's blessings and begins to complain about what amounts to a tiny inconvenience and blows it up to major proportions.

If the believer keeps his head, it does not take much to see how recklessly Satan is willing to overplay his hand at this sorry game. Actually, in playing down God's love, Satan puts up a colossal bluff because he has nothing with which to back up his claims. The moment you dare to call his bluff, his play collapses.

God's love is so evident, so altogether incontrovertible, that Satan hasn't a leg to stand on when you remind him of it.

Just point to Calvary and the magnificent demonstration of God's love in giving Christ to die for us because He loved us (John 3:16; Romans 5:5; 8:31-39).

Satan's lie must vanish when the cross of Christ is faced, even as snowflakes melt away before the warm sun. His scurrilous charge evaporates as the gift of eternal life is bestowed upon the sinner who reposes faith in Christ's atoning work. His base calumny becomes more monstrous as we realize that "every good thing bestowed and every perfect gift is from above, coming down from the Father of lights, with whom there is no variation, or shifting shadow" (James 1:17; NASB).

3

HOW SECURE IS THE SAINT?

In dealing with the subject of what Satan and demons can do to a genuinely born-again Christian, it is of the utmost importance to face the question of just how secure the saint is. The issue would be vital if the question involved only the problem of sin in the saint's life. It is even more indispensable since special study is to be given to the consideration of how far Satan and demonic powers can operate in the regenerated heart when sin is yielded to and followed.

A further reason exists as to why the question of just how secure the saint is must be explored: ignorance and error exist among believers concerning this issue. This is true even when the question is more or less limited to the saint's sin problem. It is greatly accentuated when this problem is further related to the role Satan and demons may play when a believer persists in serious, and even scandalous, sin.

SAINTHOOD AND SECURITY

It is amazing how different man's concept of sainthood is from God's. You mention the word "saint," and immediately people think of some super holy person whose life is characterized by great self-denial and good works.

Strangely enough, when you go to the Bible this idea of sainthood does not exist. In Scripture "the term never indicates personal character or worthiness." A social class of super holy people like Saint Peter, Saint Paul, or Saint John is just not found in the Bible, much less the concept that gave birth to the roster of canonized, extrabiblical, so-called "saints" that adorns the pages of the church's history.

The Bible term "saint" is a word derived from the same root in Greek as "holy" or "sanctified." It is employed sixty-two times in the New Testament to designate the believer.[2] Always it denotes what the Christian is in Christ, never what he is or accomplishes in himself.

Contrary to man's definition, God centers sainthood in Christ alone. Sinful, lost man becomes a saint through faith in the Savior as his sin-bearer. Saved by grace through faith (Ephesians 2:8-9), the believer is placed "in Christ" by the Holy Spirit. This becomes the believer's position, or sphere, in which God sees him.

Sainthood, as God sees it, is based on position, not experience. It is a static, unchangeable placement, a present reality rather than a future prospect. "Being already set apart unto God in Christ, all Christians are now by so much saints, from the moment they are saved."[3].

The biblical idea of sainthood is based entirely upon what God has done for the sinner in saving him, not upon what the saved sinner does or may do for God. The saved sinner may and, of course, should do great things for God. But none of these great things can make a believer one iota more a saint.

A believer is a saint, reckoned so by God, at the moment he is saved. Sainthood is realized on the very same basis as salvation, "by grace . . . through faith; and that not of yourselves, it is the gift of God; not as a result of works, that no one should boast" (Ephesians 2:8-9; NASB).

Salvation constitutes us saints. Works or achievements, no matter how good or great, do not make us saints. God declares us saints on the basis of what He has done for us, not on what we do for Him or for others.

Saints are therefore secure. God *declares* us saved and saints (Ephesians 1:1). Who, including Satan and demons, can declare us otherwise (Romans 8:31-39)? God *sees* us as saved and saints in Christ (Philippians 1:1; Colossians 1:12). Who can or dare see us in any other sphere? If they did, never could it affect God's seeing, only theirs.

Therefore, all believers are saints (1 Corinthians 1:2), and all saints are safe and secure in Christ insofar as their salvation and eternal destiny are concerned. The devil and the demons know this. It is high time all believers know it. To not know it or to doubt it is to play into the devil's hand and listen to his lie.

SAINTHOOD AND SIN

HOW CAN A SAINT SIN?

If a "saint" is "a holy one," or "one sanctified," how can he sin? So contradictory does the concept of a "sinning saint" appear that many believers adopt the notion that the old nature can and should be rooted out or eradicated in an experience of sanctification subsequent to salvation. Others insist that the concept that a saint can sin is valid. "But," they say, "the sinning saint forfeits his salvation."

The Scriptures plainly present the fact that not only can the saint sin, but that no saint, no matter how holy in life, can completely avoid sinning. Since the experiences of the holiest people of God back up the biblical teaching, it will do no good to try to circumvent what God declares to be true.

But how can the difficulty be solved? How can one whom God sees to be holy and calls a saint be unholy in the sense of committing sin? The answer is to be found in Christ's saving work as it is applied to the sinner who appropriates its benefits by faith. The moment a lost sinner reposes faith in the Savior by believing the gospel (1 Corinthians 15:3-4), he is saved. From God's side, this presents God as viewing the saved sinner from that instant as united to Christ. From then on he is said to be "in Christ" (declared more than 150 times in the New Testament).

Viewing the saved sinner "in Christ" simply means that the infinitely *holy* God, from the moment of salvation, looks upon him solely as being united to His Son. God sees him, therefore, in all the holiness and infinite perfections of His Son, whose very righteousness is imputed, or reckoned, to the believing sinner (Philippians 3:9; 2 Corinthians 5:21).

It is at this point that confusion is interjected in the minds of so many believers. They fail to see that this is *positional* truth—truth that applies to the mind and reckoning of God, and concerns the eternal and unchangeable placement of the believer in Christ as the result of Christ's redemptive work on the cross.

This *positional* truth must be differentiated from and yet related to *experiential* truth. The latter has to do with the believer's comprehending and appropriating positional truth by faith, thereby making it realizable in his actual experience.

How can a saint sin? He is made a saint by God's grace, given an eternal and unforfeitable placement in Christ, and declared saved and safe in the Savior. He is, therefore, a saint because he is saved, not because he lives saintly or could do or be anything to be saved and thus become a saint, or do or be anything to keep saved and thus continue as a saint.

But will not this *position* of sainthood guarantee an *experience* of sainthood? Only as the position of sainthood is understood and reckoned upon in faith (Romans 6:11). Faith in our position of sainthood in Christ conveys the benefits of sainthood into our experience.

Saints can and do sin when they fail to know and depend on their position of sainthood. Many saints do not know their placement as saints (Romans 6:1-10). Many who do know of it do not believe it and thus constantly fail to convert its benefits into daily living (Romans 6:11).

In addition to these facts, the saint has the old sin nature within alongside the new nature. The old nature is prone to sin and does sin unless constantly reckoned in the place of death. Because many saints do not reckon it dead, they sin. The apostle warns: "Let not sin therefore reign in your mortal body" (Romans 6:12). The admonition expresses the possibility of sin (personified) reigning through the believer's body. These facts explain the anomaly of a "sinning saint."

WHAT HAPPENS TO A SINNING SAINT?

Saints, then, as has been pointed out, not only can but do sin unless they appropriate victory in their placement in Christ. Moreover, they can sin immorally and scandalously if they recklessly give in to the old nature and seriously grieve and quench the indwelling Spirit (Ephesians 4:30; 1 Thessalonians 5:19).

God deals with the sinning saint as a child in the divine family. He corrects and chastens (1 Corinthians 11:32), and in severe cases He "scourges" (Hebrews 12:6). The Greek word means "to flog" or "to whip severely."[4] The Father lays the lash on the wastrel son who plays the prodigal. The lash He uses may be physical weakness, sickness, or, in severest cases, premature physical death (1 Corinthians 11:30). He employs Satan and the powers of darkness as His whip (1 Corinthians 5:5).

The purely human conclusion is that such scandalously sinning saints "lose their salvation." But divine wisdom has established that no saint can ever lose his sainthood; no one saved can ever be unsaved.

God "canonizes" His saints (Romans 8:31-39). Never does He "uncanonize" them, because canonization is based wholly on what God has done for them in Christ and not on anything good or bad that they have done or ever could do in themselves. It is pure folly to imagine that man can "uncanonize" those whom God "canonizes" (cf. John 10:27-29).

Even the sinning saint cannot "uncanonize" himself. Canonization is *wholly* the work and will of God. Therefore, man can no more canonize than he can uncanonize God's saints.

The very purpose of God's employing the powers of darkness to whip His sinning saints is not that they may go to hell. Quite the opposite is declared: "That the spirit *may be saved* in the day of the Lord Jesus" (1 Corinthians 5:1-5). True, a saint's body may suffer death at the hands of Satan, demons, and demon-driven men (cf. Matthew 10:28; 1 Corinthians 5:5; 1 John 5:16). However, Satan, demons, and wicked men can never touch the redeemed soul and spirit.

At death "the spiritual body" (the immaterial part of the saint) goes to be with the Lord (2 Corinthians 5:8). There it awaits the resurrection (Philippians 1:23; 1 Thessalonians 4:17), when it will be reunited with the body, then raised from death and glorified (made deathless and adapted to eternal life in the spirit world).

It is concluded, then, that sinning saints never lose their salvation (1 Corinthians 11:30-32). Nor will they ever land in hell (1 Corinthians 5:5). However, by their sin they do open up themselves to the powers of darkness to harass, despoil, and enslave them, besides doing them other harm, even to killing their physical bodies (1 John 5:16; cf. Matthew 10:28).

HOW CAN A SINNING SAINT BE SANCTIFIED?

Many Christians, ill-taught in the Word of God, cry out, "A sinning saint can not be sanctified. He loses his sanctification when he sins."

While it is true that a sinning saint loses his experience of sanctification when he sins, he can *never* lose his sanctified position before God. This is as assured as his position as a saint because it is based not upon anything he could be or do but entirely upon what Christ is and has done for him in saving him (1 Corinthians 1:2; 6:11).

Sanctification, like salvation, is both a position and an experience of that position. You may forfeit the experience but never the position. Likewise, sin affects the saint's experience, but it can never change his placement before God in Christ (Ephesians 1:3-12). The Corinthian believers were all saints (1 Corinthians 1:1-2), yet they were living in various sins (cf. 5:1).

Similarly, Satan and demonic powers may operate upon the saint's experience (Ephesians 6:10-20). But they can never alter his placement before God in Christ (Colossians 2:15; 1 Peter 3:22). This is secured by God's grace and power through the redemptive efficacy of Christ's finished work on the cross (Romans 8:32-37). This is precisely why Christ's victory at Calvary over sin and the powers of darkness is so superlatively grand and complete (Romans 8:38).

THE BIBLICAL BASIS FOR SECURITY

SECURE IN THE FATHER'S LOVE

The revealed Word of God declares that those whom Christ saves, He saves eternally.[5] Nowhere in the Bible is it even suggested that God ever takes back the free gift of salvation from those to whom He gives it. Nor is it ever once remotely hinted that the life that constitutes the gift is anything but eternal and can ever be terminated by anyone, including the devil and the demons.[6]

The positive doctrine of security rests solidly upon the accomplishment of God's grace manifested in Christ's redemptive work.[7] The believer is saved and safe because his salvation is not merely God's afterthought, some sudden impulse of the divine mind to rescue man after sin engulfed the race at the fall (Romans 8:29-30). On the contrary, security rests upon God's eternal purposes of sovereign grace. Gloriously God chose us in Christ "before the foundation of the world" and "predestinated us unto the adoption of children by Jesus Christ to himself" (Ephesians 1:4-6). This grand operation in behalf of poor, undone sinners is totally apart from human merit or work (Ephesians 2:8-9).

Everywhere upon the pages of revealed truth gleams God's sovereign promise, unconditionally granting eternal salvation to everyone who believes in Christ (John 3:16; 5:24). What God promises He is of course able to do. He records His unchangeable will for the joy and assurance of all who believe (Romans 8:29-30).

Scripture declares that God, being free from every barrier to forgive man's sin, is able to keep in His love and power all whom He redeems through Christ (John 10:29; Romans 4:21; Jude 1:24). In fact, God's infinite love is displayed in His eternal purpose and assures the fulfillment of all His plans for the redeemed (John 6:37-40).

The wonder of God's love for His redeemed is set forth simply but powerfully by the apostle Paul in Romans. If God loved lost men enough to send His son to die for them when they were "sinners" and "enemies," how much more will He cherish and keep those whom He has justified and reconciled by His redeeming grace (Romans 5:8-11)?

The Father's eternal purpose and sovereign promise, as well as His infinite power and love, gloriously assure that he who trusts Christ as His Savior can never lose the salvation God works in his life.

But in forgiving sin and providing eternal salvation, God is not merely acting in love. He is acting with infinite righteousness as well. Every demand of the divine holiness has been completely met by the death of Christ in that He died for the sins of the whole world (1 John 2:2). Those who challenge the eternal security of the believer cannot at the same time avoid challenging God's righteousness.

SECURE THROUGH THE SON'S REDEMPTIVE WORK

When Jesus died on the cross, He vicariously bore *all* the believer's sins—past, present, and future. He took the sinner's place in death. He died as his substitute. His death is the sufficient answer to the condemning power of sin (Romans 8:34). Salvation and safekeeping depend only on Christ's sacrifice and merit. Through His atoning work all condemnation is removed forever (John 3:18; Romans 8:1).

Christ's resurrection was the seal of the all-sufficiency of His death as a vicarious atonement for sin. It made possible God's gift of eternal life (John 3:16; 10:28). Since this life is the life of the risen Christ (Colossians 2:12; 3:1-4), it is as eternal as He is eternal. The very fact that God's gift is eternal life means that it is incapable of dissolution.

Union with Christ by baptism with the Spirit places the believer in the sphere of life that is as unending as Christ Himself is unending. Taken out of the federal headship of the first Adam, the believer is placed "in Christ" under the federal headship of the last Adam (1 Corinthians 15:20-22, 45-48).

Our head is the last Adam (the resurrected Christ), who cannot fall. It is an utter impossibility for the weakest saint who is united to Him to fall. God sees every saved person as a saint because he is united to Christ, and God sees him "in Christ" now and forever (2 Corinthians 5:17).

SECURE THROUGH THE SON'S PRESENT INTERCESSION

On the basis of His finished redemptive work on the cross, followed by His resurrection and ascension, Christ conducts a present ministry of intercession in glory. This prayer is a continuation of that which was begun on earth in anticipation of His redemptive sacrifice on Calvary (John 17:9-12, 15, 20-21). Christ is now interceding for His own who are in the world (Luke 22:32; Romans 8:34). His heavenly intercession guarantees that they will be kept saved forever (John 14:19; Romans 5:10; Hebrews 7:25).

SECURE THROUGH THE SON'S PRESENT ADVOCACY

This aspect of Christ's present ministry in heaven deals with the believer's sin. In the light of God's infinite holiness, the believer's sin in every instance merits eternal condemnation. If Christ, as the believer's Advocate, did not continually plead the efficacy of His own blood before the throne of God, that judgment would necessarily be executed (1 John 2:1-2; Romans 8:34; Hebrews 9:24).

Those who deny the believer's security must deny either the efficacy or the unbroken continuity of Christ's advocacy. But Scripture declares both. It explicitly assures us that Christ "ever lives to make intercession" and that "he is able also to save them to the uttermost [completely] that come unto God by him" (Hebrews 7:25).

SECURE THROUGH THE SPIRIT'S REGENERATING WORK

By the Spirit's operation in regeneration the believers are constituted sons and made "joint-heirs [of God] with Christ" (John 1:13; 3:3-6; Romans 8:16-17). Being born of God, the regenerated souls partake of the divine nature, which is eternal as God is eternal and is never removed or annulled (2 Peter 1:4).

The new birth, accordingly, is an irreversible process and entirely the work of the Holy Spirit. It is as once-for-all and unrepeatable as one's natural birth. Being an operation of God and not man and being entirely on the principle of grace, there is no ground or valid reason why it should not continue forever.

SECURE THROUGH THE SPIRIT'S BAPTIZING WORK

The moment the believer is regenerated he is simultaneously baptized by the Spirit into union with Christ and the church, the Body of Christ (1 Corinthians 6:17; 12:13; Galatians 3:27). The resulting new position "in Christ" is a vital and permanent placement. This new sphere contrasts with the old sphere of sin and condemnation "in Adam." It represents the new sphere of righteousness and justification "in Christ." With a wholly new position and relationship, the believer becomes a part of the new creation (2 Corinthians 5:17-18).

But perhaps the most thrilling aspect of the new position in Christ is that the believer is "accepted in the beloved" (Ephesians 1:6). This means that "the child of God is as secure as the One in whom he is and in whom he stands."[8] In fact, God sees all who are "in Christ" in all the perfection and delight of His only begotten Son, our Lord and Savior. The reason is simple. The believer is "in Him," and God never sees him in any other position or relationship than in that of His own beloved Son.

SECURE THROUGH THE SPIRIT'S INDWELLING

When a person is saved, the Holy Spirit takes up residence in his body. In the present age the indwelling presence of the Spirit is a permanent possession of every believer (John 7:37-39; Romans 5:5; 8:9; 1 Corinthians 2:12; 6:19). Scriptural intimation points to the conclusion that in pre-Pentecostal times not all believers enjoyed the permanent indwelling, even though they were saved by faith that glimpsed the coming Savior (Psalm 51:ll; 1 Samuel 16:14; Romans 3:25).

But in the present age the Holy Spirit indwells the believer permanently (John 14:16). That the believer's body, even though corrupt and sinful, is the temple of God demonstrates God's unswerving purpose to bring to consummation what He has begun in saving the believer.

Although the believer may grieve the indwelling Spirit by sin, the Spirit can never be grieved away (Ephesians 4:30). Although the believer may quench the Spirit by disobedience (1 Thessalonians 5:19), the Spirit can never be extinguished. In fact, Scripture makes its appeal to the believer for a holy walk in God's will on the basis of the fact that the Spirit permanently indwells him and that his salvation is unforfeitably sure.

SECURE THROUGH THE SPIRIT'S SEALING

The indwelling Spirit Himself is the seal (Ephesians 1:13-14; 4:30; 2 Corinthians 1:22). A seal is a mark of protection that guarantees security. A letter is sealed so that its contents remain inviolable. So God seals His own with a seal that can never be broken and will remain intact until the redeemed body is glorified either by rapture or by resurrection.

Since the sealing is an act of God, no creature—including satan, demons, or man—can break it. It is backed up by the purpose, the power, the love, the holiness, and the faithfulness of God the Father. It is bestowed on the basis of the death, burial, resurrection, and ascension of the Son. It is effected by God's outpoured gift of the Spirit.

As a work of God, the sealing signifies the safety and security of the one sealed. The redeemed one is "sealed until God completes His purpose to present the believer faultless in heaven," constituting "another evidence that a believer once saved is always saved."[9]

SECURE THROUGH THE SPIRIT'S FILLING

Every believer is positionally filled with the Spirit the moment he is saved. This means God places him and sees him "in Christ," which is the sphere of spiritual fullness when he is saved. In fact, he is viewed as complete "in Christ," in whom "all the fulness of Deity dwells" (Colossians 2:9-10; NASB). Experiential filling of the Spirit is based upon this positional fullness and is to be "a continuous, and ever-expanding experience of the Christian life."[10]

Positional fullness, on the other hand, is a static, unalterable placement. It is a vital, inseparable part of salvation. Hence, it is entirely on the basis of God's grace in response to faith in Christ's redemptive work, as salvation is.

Since *all* believers are positionally filled with the Spirit, and because they are brought into the realm of spiritual fullness "in Christ" by salvation, this furnishes another evidence of the believer's eternal safety and security.

SECURE IN OUR SO GREAT SALVATION

Salvation and safekeeping have of necessity been treated as separate divine undertakings. This is an adaptation to human understanding and the usual ways of speaking. Actually, Scripture recognizes no such distinction. Salvation is a glorious whole composed of inseparable parts. The parts may and can be isolated and separated in order that finite minds might comprehend something of the infinite complexity and wonder of our "so great salvation" (Hebrews 2:3).

Actually, when God saves a sinner, the saving operation is wrought as a whole, instantly and eternally. Moreover, considered as a whole, salvation by its very nature provides eternal security for its recipients.

It is God's work, not man's. It rests on the power and faithfulness of God, not on man's strength or faithfulness. It is all of grace, totally by faith, and not at all by works. If salvation were by works or if it were a reward of faith, it might be understandable how a believer's security might be called in question. But resting upon what God has promised and performed in behalf of a lost and ruined race, the believer can rejoice in a finished and absolutely efficacious redemption.

Sin, Satan, demons, and wicked men are powerless to destroy what Jesus Christ accomplished by His death and resurrection. Every believer can rejoice in his security. With Paul he can be "confident of this very thing, that he which hath begun a good work" in him "will perform it until the day of Jesus Christ" (Philippians 1:6; cf. John 6:37; 17:15-16; Romans 8:29). Satan and demons know what some of God's people do not know. Not one of the redeemed, blood-washed, and saved believers shall ever be lost and fail to enter heaven.

These words of our Savior Himself are decisive: "My sheep hear my voice, and I know them, and they follow me:

and I give unto them eternal life; and they shall never perish, neither shall any man pluck them out of my hand. My Father, which gave them me, is greater than all; and no man is able to pluck them out of my Father's hand" (John 10:27-29).

SECURE IN OUR ASSURANCE OF SALVATION

The truth of security gives assurance, or personal confidence, in a present salvation. Assurance rests first and foremost upon God's declarations, revealed in His Word. To be saved, one must hear and believe God's Word. Specifically, one must believe the gospel: that God saves sinners on the basis of simple faith in Christ's finished redemptive work (1 Corinthians 15:1-4).

But many who have believed the gospel and are saved still lack assurance of salvation. Personal conviction of having a present salvation springs from believing the Word in its larger context (1 John 5:13). The promises of Scripture, with the exposition it contains of the meaning of Christ's work on the cross, furnish the basis on which assurance is built (John 6:37; Romans 1:16; 10:13).

Those who reject the truth of the believer's security can never realize the joy and stability that assurance gives to the Christian life. Even though they possess a valid born-again experience, they tend to substitute feelings, works, or their own thoughts for faith.

Confidence that one is saved and forever safe in the Beloved is the only sound ground for victory over the world, the flesh, and the devil. Believing that we are what we are in Christ assures a triumphal life that redounds to the glory of God and the blessing of man.

PERILS FACING SAINTS WHO LACK ASSURANCE

Many saints of God in the church today possess no real sense of their security in Christ. The reason is simple. They subscribe to no adequate biblical doctrine of security and

hence have no genuine and abiding experience of its blessing in their lives. Theoretically, they hold to the absolute sufficiency of Christ's saving work on the cross. Practically,
however, they balk at its full ramifications in Christian
conduct.

Strangely enough, many of them are dedicated and very
active and useful in the Lord's work. Their lack of conviction
on the believer's security, or, in some instances, their open
opposition to this doctrine, is not revealed until they face a
problem such as serious sin and backsliding. Then the danger of their view appears.

In such instances insecure believers who fall into serious sin and backsliding imagine that they have forfeited their
salvation. By so doing, they rule out the possibility of obeying
the injunction to "be strong in the Lord, and in the power of
his might" (Ephesians 6:10). This actually means that they
cut out from under their feet the ground on which they are to
stand (if they stand) against the enemy, because their
strength is not from the Lord but in their position in the Lord.

Not counting on their position of strength in union with
Christ and not drawing their power from that position, they
have no ground on which to stand against the enemy. As a
result, they are unable to "put on the whole armour of God,
that . . . [they] may be able to stand against the wiles of the
devil" (Ephesians 6:11-20). The upshot is that the powers of
darkness can advance at will, deceiving and oppressing.
Commonly, the enemy attempts to delude his victim into believing that God will never forgive him and that therefore his
life and testimony are ruined. Or worse still, the deceiver will
whisper in the believer's ear that he has committed the "unpardonable sin" and is irretrievably doomed to hell.

Demonic powers will make every effort to paint the situation so black that in the absence of unwavering faith in the
absolute efficacy of Christ's finished work on the cross to
save the believing sinner for time and eternity, the sinning
saint lays himself open to demonic imposture. Under demon

impulsion he may yield to deep depression or, in extreme cases, even to suicide.

Several years ago a young man, a genuine believer who was severely afflicted by demonic powers, came to me for counseling. His case was so severe that periodically he spoke in another voice and under another personality, falling into such deep depression that he not only doubted his salvation but at such times contemplated suicide. The state of utter hopelessness into which he had been plunged was due to the fact that extended psychiatric tests and treatments had not alleviated his condition one iota.

At the time he knew little about Satan and nothing about demons and their power to harass and disturb human personality. There seemed to be no way of escape from his intolerable misery. He felt he just could not face life in the wretched condition to which he had been reduced.

When I explained the deliverance possible for him by virtue of his position in Christ and described the nature of demons and how these vile, evil beings were undoubtedly oppressing him and causing his trouble, I could actually see the terrible danger that gripped him give way and begin to vanish. A glimmer of hope entered his heart and was reflected in the change on his saddened face.

Under my direction and with an open Bible, he carefully studied my book *Demons in the World Today.* Through this means the Holy Spirit was able to ground him in the truth of the glorious security of the saint in Christ and the efficacy of believing prayer to repel the demonic powers devastating his life.

PERILS FACING THE SAINT
SEEKING A DEEPER SPIRITUAL EXPERIENCE

It is, of course, highly commendable that a child of God should have a hunger for a closer walk with the Lord and a desire for a greater experience of God's power. Seeking such an experience can certainly result in tremendous blessing if it is sought in accord with God's Word and guided by faith in Christ's finished redemptive work, in full realization of what salvation is and what it brings to the believer.

On the other hand, seeking a deeper experience on the basis of feeling and physical manifestations instead of faith, and apart from an accurate comprehension of the content and scope of "our common salvation" (Jude 1:3; NASB) that springs from Calvary, can be dangerous. Such a believer, seeking God's best, by the very nature of the case becomes a prime target of Satan, who will do all in his power to thwart the seeker's high quest for a closer walk with God. Unless the seeking saint proceeds upon sound scriptural principles, he runs the grave risk of falling into Satan's snare and coming under the delusive power of wandering spirits (1 Timothy 4:1).

In an era of charismatic confusion, Christian counselors are frequently being confronted with believers who have become completely disoriented spiritually as a result of being misled in the matter of the filling of the Spirit. A Christian woman, having read *Demons in the World Today,* wrote to me for help. A believer for many years, she had been nurtured in the truth of the Word concerning the believer's security and his position before God in his placement in Christ. When a keen desire for a deeper walk with God developed in her soul, she strayed from the simple Bible way to be filled with the Spirit—by faith in what the believer is in Christ (cf. 2 Corinthians 11:3-4)—and began to be lured away to seek an experience beyond salvation evidenced by the physical manifestation of speaking in tongues. For years she sought this experience avidly and determinedly, doing everything she was told to do and submitting to everything she thought she should submit to, including the laying on of hands.

Finally the tongues came. But the blessing was a mixed one. The ecstatic joy of giving vent to the tongues was followed by abject gloom. The emotional high was succeeded by a spiritual low. Worse still, peace vanished and she lost all sense of security. She found herself invaded by alien spirits who took her into the deepest type of depression and goaded her on to commit suicide.

"When the tormentors begin their work on my mind and body," she declared, "they blaspheme and talk back."

I directed this harassed believer to a prayer group whose members had had much experience and success in conducting spiritual battle for deliverance of the demonically oppressed. Her road back to spiritual health has been long and arduous. Her fate stands as a sober warning to all believers who lose sight of their completeness in Christ and who seek for spiritual fullness anywhere else than in Him alone.

A Christian counselor friend told me of a similar case regarding a woman who came to him for counsel. A staunch believer for years, she recently attended a charismatic meeting and was told that unless she had spoken in tongues, she had never been filled with the Spirit. Upon receiving the laying on of hands, she fell into a trancelike state of unconsciousness. Recovering, she discovered to her dismay that all the peace she ever had had vanished. She began to be tormented with thoughts of being lost. Her everyday life became filled with strange spiritual onslaughts and temptations to such a degree that she concluded that the laying on of hands could not have been of God.

After my friend talked with her, reviewing the fullness of her salvation in Christ and the unchangeable glory and completeness of her position in Him, she saw the mistake she had made. She asked God to forgive her for distrusting what Christ had done for her and for forgetting what she was in union with Him.

Gloriously she regained her assurance of salvation. She discovered in a new and thrilling way that, being in Christ, she was in the sphere of spiritual fullness. She found that all she needed was to know her position of fullness in her Savior and to trust Him moment by moment for the manifestation of that fullness in her everyday experiences. When she did this, she was blessedly filled with the Spirit. As she continued to believe what she was in Christ, she was continually filled. Joyfully she realized that she had found the secret of the fullness of spiritual blessing.

Her joy was the more abundant as the fact dawned upon her that this was exactly what the Holy Spirit had been teaching all along through the apostle Paul in Romans 6:11: "Likewise reckon ye also yourselves to be dead indeed unto sin, but alive unto God through [in union with] Jesus Christ our Lord." At the same time she saw how serious her mistake had been in seeking spiritual fullness anywhere else than in Christ alone and in the salvation He gives at the moment the gospel of grace is believed.

4

CAN A DEMON INVADE A SAINT?

In an era of rampant occultism and increased demon activity, great perplexity exists among many Christians concerning the extent to which Satan and demonic powers can enter and control the life of a believer. Many Christians naively assume that the potential of satanic power in the life of the regenerated is practically nil. They live in a sort of fool's paradise, imagining that becoming Christians magically shields them from satanic attack or demonic invasion.[1]

Other believers maintain a more realistic view. They are fully convinced that satanic powers may not only tempt and attack but that, if they are not repulsed, they may affect the saint's life and do serious harm in his experience. They may influence him, delude him, despoil him. Always, however, they attack the saint from without, but never exercising total control over him. To such people the possibility of a born-again believer being invaded by one or more demons is preposterous and, in their view, unbiblical.[2]

A third class of believers holds to what seems to me the most realistic view. Grievously sinning saints (and such there are) may go beyond the old nature. In cases of serious, persistent, scandalous sin, such as gross immorality or participation in occultism or occult religionism, demons may exercise control over the believer for a time until his sin is confessed and forsaken and deliverance from the evil powers is gained.[3]

THE ISSUE AT STAKE

The question that presses for an answer is clear. *Can a believer be invaded by one or more demons?* If so, is such invasion by one or more demons to be viewed as demon possession or is the phenomenon of possession a deeper and more servile degree of devil domination? What is meant by "being demonized?" What is the distinction between demon influence, demon inhabitation, and demon possession? Can a believer ever become demonized?

DEMON INFLUENCE DEFINED

Demon influence is the action of demonic powers working to corrupt a person. It may be of various degrees of severity, depending on the resistance the believer offers the satanic onslaughts (cf. James 4:7). If he fails to "stand against the wiles of the devil" (Ephesians 6:11) and yields to this pressure, the enemy takes all the territory allowed him. Satanic forces operate upon this principle: "We go as far as we are permitted to go."

When evil spiritual forces are allowed to operate unchecked upon the mind, the will, the emotions, and the bodily appetites, influence imperceptibly becomes greater and greater. Demonic pressure grows stronger and stronger. If demonic attack is not resisted, the result is demonic invasion of the personality. This condition eventuates in still more serious forms of enslavement.

Demon influence, at least in its milder forms, is extremely common among the regenerate, not to mention its all but universal prevalence among the unsaved (Ephesians 2:1-2; 2 Corinthians 4:3-4). In an age of increasing moral laxity and spiritual lawlessness, the more serious forms of demon influence are becoming more prevalent among Christian people.

To an alarming degree, regenerated people are becoming imperiled by the phenomenal growth of the cults. On every hand, they are facing the subtle satanic strategy to substitute demonized religion for pure, biblical, historical Christianity.[4] With the breakdown of morals, Christians are beset with demon influences with which they have never before been confronted—in their own personal lives as well as in the home, the church, the school, and in society as a whole.

Demon Influence and Christian Experience

It must be remembered that the obedient-to-the-Word, Spirit-filled believer is shielded from demon influence. He strengthens himself in his unchangeable position of victory in Christ. He enjoys the power and might made available to him in that position. He is able to conduct a successful warfare against his spiritual foes, so they are therefore unable to trick him (Ephesians 6:10-12).

Many Christians, however, do not wage a successful battle against the enemy. Instead, they parley or compromise with evil. They fellowship with darkness or unite with error. They yield to the old Adamic nature and through carnality and sin open the door to evil spirits to affect their thinking and their conduct.

Pastors and Christian counselors most frequently encounter demonic influence among people who come to them for help. Less severe cases are easily corrected as the believer sees that his trouble stems from failure to know and to act upon his position in Christ (Romans 6:11). When he begins to exercise faith in what Christ has done for him and what he is in Christ, his problems begin to dissolve as he banishes ignorance and unbelief from his thinking.

More severe cases of demonic influence are not as easily handled. A believer persistently yields to a besetting sin and gradually discovers that he is unable to confess it and turn away from it. But when the sin is clearly demonic, he also finds himself unwilling to do so.

A believer with a tendency toward lascivious thoughts yields to the temptation to indulge the old nature by reading pornographic literature. He soon finds his mind polluted by vile imaginations whenever he attempts to read the Bible or pray or perform any spiritual service for God. Strong demonic influence on his mind stifles every effort in Christian living and serving.

Unless the believer at this point obtains spiritual help from the Word of God through a preacher of the Word or a Christian counselor so that he is brought to a state of confession and renunciation of the sin, he runs the risk of going on to a more severe state of demonic control. The lascivious tendency grows into an overpowering obsession as unclean thoughts overmaster the mind. Open immorality or sexual perversion is the result, and ministry and witness for God are destroyed.

Any sin of the flesh or spirit may be indulged in this manner and pass through the various stages of demonic influence. But in every instance the demonic power is brought to bear upon the personality from without. The demon does not actually enter the body and operate from within. This type of demon subjection from without undoubtedly constitutes the category in which the great bulk of Christian experience connected with demon activity is to be classified. Comparatively few truly born-again believers apparently go beyond strong demon influence. In fact, so few do so that many Christians maintain that none do. Many insist that no genuinely regenerated believer can be invaded by demon powers.

CAN DEMONS INVADE A BELIEVER'S LIFE?

In the so-called age of Aquarius, which since 1970 has designated the present era of occultism and demonism, the question of whether demons can invade and control the life of a Christian has pressed to the fore. Great naiveté and uncertainty exist in Christian circles concerning the answer.

Those who hold that a truly regenerated person cannot possibly be invaded by demons argue somewhat along these lines: The believer has been delivered from the power of Satan and his demons (Colossians 1:12-13; Ephesians 2:1-3). Christ's purpose was to destroy the works of the devil (1 John 3:8). The Christian has the full equipment to conduct a successful warfare against the enemy (Ephesians 6:11-18), and the armor provided is for external, not internal, foes.

The Holy Spirit, who inhabits a believer, precludes the believer being inhabited by a demon spirit (1 Corinthians 6:19; 1 John 4.4). The internal struggle of the believer is revealed to be a warfare between the Spirit and the flesh, not between the Holy Spirit and demon spirits (Romans 6:1–7:25; Galatians 5:17).

It is true, of course, that the believer has been delivered from the power of Satan and demons. He also has been delivered from the power of sin. But does that mean he may not fall under its power if he does not count on his deliverance? Likewise, he may through his old nature succumb to the temporary control of Satan and demons unless he reckons on his deliverance.

Christ's purpose was indeed to destroy the works of the devil, and He certainly accomplished this by His death and resurrection. But does this mean that Satan and demons have as yet been relegated to the abyss or that they are not now free to tempt and overcome a believer?

A Christian, to be sure, has the full armor of God to wage a victorious war against Satan and demons. But does he always do so? Will Satan and demons hesitate to press their attack and draw back from invading the life if resistance is not offered? Indeed, it is true that the believer's armor is for external and not for internal foes. But if the Christian fails to use his armor, will the foe stop short of invading the believer's citadel? If he does invade, this is precisely why the believer may become enslaved and need to call on Christian warriors to come to his rescue in prayer battle if he is ever to be delivered from Satan's snare into which he has been "taken captive by him at his will" (2 Timothy 2:26). He thus becomes the victim of an enslavement from which he is unable to free himself without help in prayer.

In such a case the normal struggle between the flesh and the Spirit (Galatians 5:17) ceases. The believer is invaded and overrun by the enemy, who, like any invading foe, does not permit the use of weapons of any sort by the citizens of the country overrun. As a result there is no struggle, only enforced submission and subservience.

The Holy Spirit indwelling the believer ungrieved by sin (Ephesians 4:30) and unquenched by disobedience (1 Thessalonians 5:19) most certainly precludes invasion by a demon spirit. But who dares assert that a demon spirit will not invade the life of a believer in which the Holy Spirit has been grieved by serious and persistent sin and quenched by flagrant disobedience?

The demon enters, it is true, as a squatter and not as an owner or a guest or as one who has a right there. He comes in as an intruder and as an invader and enemy. But come he does if the door is opened by serious and protracted sin.

Satan and his minions have no legal right to enter, for the Christian's body belongs only to God both by creation and redemption (Psalm 100:3; 1 Corinthians 6:19-20). But as a squatter, defined as "one who settles on land without right or title or payment of rent,"[5] a demon can come in and settle down for a time. He will leave only if he is forcibly ejected by faith and prayer on the part of Christian warriors who know their position and resources in Christ and use their prayer armor effectively.

The claim that the Holy Spirit could not dwell in the same body with an evil spirit overlooks an important theological observation. It might with equal cogency be asked how the Holy Spirit can dwell in our bodies, which are still possessed of the old nature and therefore subject to sin. Yet He does because of our redemption and the presence of the new nature.

In His atoning death, Christ secured a judicial sentence against "sin in the flesh" (Romans 5:10; 8:3) so that the infinite holiness of God is not in the least compromised by the Holy Spirit's indwelling saved sinners. Similarly, the Spirit's infinite holiness is not compromised by an invading demon spirit.

It must be stressed that demons cannot indwell a Christian in the same sense as the Holy Spirit. God's Spirit enters a believer at salvation, permanently, never to leave (John 14:16). A demon, by contrast, enters as a squatter and an intruder and is subject to momentary eviction. A demon never rightfully or permanently indwells a saint, as the Holy Spirit does, and no demon can ever have any influence over any part of a Christian's life that is yielded to the Holy Spirit.

Moreover, the Holy Spirit indwelling the believer is omnipotent. He is greater than he (Satan and the powers of darkness) "who is in the world" (1 John 4:4; NASB). When the Christian believes and follows the Word of God and relies upon God's Spirit to keep him from sin, the powers of darkness are unable to touch him. Only as the believer fails to walk by faith does he fall into sin, which, if it is not confessed and curbed, may ultimately result in the forfeiture of the Spirit's power to shield him from demonic invasion.

One thing is certain. If anyone for one reason or another is found to be oppressed by demons, Scripture offers him the most complete deliverance through Christ's redemptive work. On the cross He "spoiled the principalities and the powers . . . made a show of them openly, triumphing over them in it" (Colossians 2:15; ASV*).

* *American Standard Version*

EXPERIENCES OF A RETIRED MILITARY MAN

A military man's experiences of demon harassment began in 1972 when he was stationed at Sheppard Air Force Base in Texas. Having served almost twenty years in the military, it was when he began to contemplate retirement to civilian life that he started to experience strange supernatural manifestations. At the time he was not a believer and did not recognize the first and many subsequent communications with the supernatural as the invasion of demonic spirits into his life.

From this point on, his existence became almost intolerable as he began to be tormented by inner voices imitating friends and acquaintances and as he became the unhappy target of many demonic schemes to distract and vex him. Having read my book *Demons in the World Today*, he wrote to me in February 1975 after he had joined a Bible-believing church and become a staunch believer. Yet he was still tormented by evil spirits. At that time he wrote,

> I do not understand the situation, but I do *know* that I believe in our Lord and Savior, Jesus Christ, and do seek to serve Him as best I can. A missionary friend from Brazil stated that he personally knew a born-again Christian who had to fend off demonic onslaughts for twelve years before receiving relief. I pray that my relief will come much sooner.

Although conversion to Christ did not remove this man's demonic problem, it put the whole matter in a different light. Not only did he then recognize who his enemy was, but, from studying God's Word, he knew that in Christ full deliverance is provided from all satanic power. In the same letter he wrote,

> I want to thank you for your concern concerning my case. In a way I have grown accustomed to the demonic harassment that I have been receiving, feeling that it would cease as time

goes by. However, my efforts to communicate with you and others regarding my experiences have provoked an increase in the activities of the spirits. Much of it is in the form of increased harassment, torment, and oppression.

This believer, as his own words show, was engaging in wishful thinking when he said he felt that the demonic harassment "would cease as time goes by." In our communication with him, however, we warned him that this was not the case. Deliverance could be his only by enlisting concentrated prayer and waging a spiritual warfare against the demonic spirits to oust them and claim victory in Christ. When he realized this fact, he determined to seek complete emancipation in group prayer.

In his personal testimony he told how hundreds of these invisible spirit beings approached and spoke to him. Most of them sought to confuse and mislead him, attempting to promote belief in reincarnation, spiritualism, or Buddhism, or to try to get him to believe that he was some sort of gifted psychic, prophet, or religious leader. Their schemes to foster heresy, apostasy, or disbelief in God were manifold and clever. He declared,

> Contrary to what some might say, or believe, these demonic spirits *can* influence, harass, and torment the true believer, as well as those who have not accepted Jesus Christ as their Savior. I know them to be able to inject thoughts which refute the Bible's teachings and which are foreign and repugnant to the born-again Christian's true beliefs.
>
> I know them to be the cause of wild and irrational thinking and behavior in myself and in others. One tactic frequently used by these evil beings involves creating a plan of action within the individual's mind, either by verbal comment or thought injection, then immediately verbalizing or interjecting counter thoughts, doubts, and different conclusions, until the human victim is thoroughly confused and mentally tormented

to the point of irrational behavior. Such is their sadistic and vile nature. . . .

Many attempts have been made to lead me astray and to cause me great physical and mental harm. A particularly vile tactic involves self-destruction. On numerous occasions these spirits sought verbally to convince me that suicide was the only answer.

Being a Christian, confident in Christ, and having direct knowledge of their presence and tactics, I am, of course, not about to give in to their threats or to accommodate their desire for my destruction. However, I am persuaded that many other human beings have.

I thank God for the strength, hope and saving grace of our Lord and Savior! Had the others known, and believed as I do, perhaps they too could have endured and their lives been salvaged.

My review of books, including the Bible, which deal with the supernatural world, indicates that much of the reported phenomena is normally perceived by a single individual. This has been generally true of my experiences. I seem to be the only person who hears these spirit beings speak, or observes or perceives the occurrence of related phenomena, though others are present.

Considering the fact that I was forty years old when these experiences began, it is certainly not an ability that I was born with. Neither is it reasonable to assume that such powers of perception were suddenly granted me in order that I might have communication with demons.

The fact that a person, sooner or later, realizes that he (or she) is the only one who hears these beings, or sees the phenomena, places him in an agonizing and frustrating position. Today's society often calls those insane who hear voices or see events or objects that others cannot.

I am sure that there have been many who were incarcerated or committed to mental institutions for making such admissions. I am also certain that there have been many who have refused to step forward and proclaim these occurrences for the very same reason.

In contrast, many have actually suffered a form of madness brought about by demons entering their lives. My earlier irrational behavior and subsequent hospitalization in the United States Soldier and Airman's Home in Washington, D.C., were certainly caused by demonic beings who invaded my life.

Some of these demons involved in my life seem more vicious and vile than others. There have been many instances in which their acts and comments seemed merely foolish and nonsensical. Some could properly be called "seducing spirits" who subtly sought to mislead, confuse, and destroy my belief in God and the Bible. Others, however, are truthfully criminals of the worst type—sadistic, malicious, and thoroughly depraved, whose intent seems to be to degrade, defile, and destroy. In fact, their activities and comments can only be described as a form of insanity—an irrational desire to torment, manipulate, and control.

It may be difficult for some to believe the Scripture's description of Lucifer's fall, because he rebelled against his Creator's will due to pride and desire for power. However, I believe every word of it. My experiences with demons have shown me how self-centered and obsessed with a desire for power many of these spirit beings are.

In their attempts to influence and manipulate my thought and behavior they have used physical and mental abuse, torture, and terror tactics. Sustained periods of harassment are contrived to prevent necessary rest and sleep, constituting an insidious assault which slowly erodes an individual's physical and mental well-being and his ability to remain rational and in control of himself.

I wonder how many other people are being harassed, tormented, and misled by these same demonic spirits that invaded my life? In one respect I was fortunate. I eventually did discover my real enemy—through coming to know my real Friend—Jesus Christ the Saviour and Deliverer, who promises me victory over these powers of darkness.

How many others are approached silently and are then afflicted, tormented, and driven to despair, even madness, not ever knowing what occurred! How many others are led to do great harm to themselves and to others! How many prison cells and mental wards are filled with people afllicted by these same enemies of God and mankind!

5

IS DEMON AFFLICTION
CONFINED TO THE UNSAVED?

No Christian who takes the Word of God seriously and who believes its testimony concerning the powers of darkness can for one moment doubt that Satan and demons do control and often harass unsaved people. It is also clearly revealed in Scripture that unsaved people may be slavishly dominated by evil spirits so that they become severely demonized. In the demonized state they become subservient to one or more demons. These evil spirits speak and act through them and may reduce them to the status of abject slaves of the devil.

A DIFFICULTY ARISES

Those who maintain, however, that no believer can be invaded by Satan or demonic powers run into a serious problem. In every case of clear-cut demon invasion they must assume that the person in question is unsaved. But the fact remains that numbers of Christians are experiencing vexing problems and grave hang-ups that manifestly go beyond natural infirmities or the struggle between the Spirit and the flesh.

A young theological student saved out of an occult-ridden family background is periodically tormented by a persistent demon. He is an active evangelist and can present Christ so effectively that people are saved under his ministry. Yet, at times, he is overwhelmed with murderous hate and afflicted with a frightful compulsion to kill another evangelist.

I once counseled with the young man. At that time he displayed one of the evidences of demon invasion—the splitting of the personality. One moment he spoke as his own self; the next he spoke as an entirely different person, as a result of the activity of the oppressing spirit. At the demon's whim the young man's thoughts and actions were reduced to chaos.

For various reasons many Christians are in terrible bondage and torment. Some are victims of disabilities that have no traceable or discernible natural cause, while others are caught in the throes of paralyzing discouragement or deep depression that has no rational explanation. Others make attempts on their lives. Some succeed in what can only be diagnosed as a demon-driven act.

In one of my pastorates the entire church was shocked when one of the members, a woman who was an earnest prayer warrior and from all evidence a genuine believer, suddenly committed suicide. One wonders if a demon so deluded that saint that she took her life.

The testimonies of numbers of Christian counselors dovetail. They have worked with scores of people who joyously confessed Jesus Christ as their Savior but who were unquestionably invaded by one or more demons. In each case the unmistakable indication of the demon's presence was discernible. There was the speaking out through the afflicted individual of another person who denied the lordship of Christ and gave allegiance to Satan.

This invading spirit either simulates the voice of the victim or speaks with an entirely different voice or even in another language. In either case it is the oppressing demon who speaks, and this is the cause of the split personality that the demon-controlled persons manifest.

Now the crux of the problem is this: A definite declaration of Scripture that no truly regenerated believer can be invaded or influenced by an evil spirit would necessitate the inescapable conclusion that all these people *were not really saved.* And this judgment of the case would have to be made in spite of the fact that they trusted and loved the Lord Jesus and gave indisputable evidence of the Holy Spirit's operation in their lives.

It is readily seen how confusing such a situation would be. Since they have believed the gospel, what else could be told them about how to be saved? If salvation is to rest on any other basis than faith in Christ, what assurance would anyone have that he is truly a child of God?

A Difficulty Solved

The truth of the matter is that the Scriptures nowhere plainly state that a true believer cannot be invaded by Satan or his demons. Of course, doctrine must always have precedence over experience. Nor can experience ever furnish a basis for biblical interpretation. Yet, if consistent experiences clash with an interpretation, the only inference possible is that there is something wrong with either the experience itself or the interpretation of the Scripture that runs counter to it. Certainly the inspired Word of God never contradicts valid experience. The sincere truth seeker must be prepared to revamp his interpretation to bring it into conformity with facts as they are.

This is exactly what I have been compelled to do in the course of the years. In *Biblical Demonology,* which was first published in 1952, the position was taken that only unbelievers are exposed to demonization.[1] But in the intervening years, numbers of letters and reports of cases of demon invasion of believers have come to me from missionaries in various parts of the world. As a result, in my study of the present-day outburst of occultism entitled *Demons in the*

World Today, which appeared in 1971, the confession is freely made that the position taken in *Biblical Demonology* "was inferred, since Scripture does not clearly settle the question."[2]

With the dawn of the age of the occult in 1970 and the widespread practice of the magical arts, the question of whether a genuine Christian can be invaded and inhabited by demonic powers has pressed itself with increased intensity upon believers. Christian people seem to divide themselves into two distinct groups. In so-called "Christian lands," believers commonly take the negative point of view. On the surface, this position seems to jibe with Scripture. Civilization, cultural progress, and the effects of preceding generations of Christian living have tended to hold down and hide the cruder forms of demon operation in humanity.

In so-called "pagan lands," where demon activity has raged unchecked for millenniums, many Christian missionaries declare that demons can and do invade and control believers who open the door by compromise and complicity with idolatry and sin. In fact, they add what is a truism among people saved out of crude heathenism, namely that a demon-harassed person often finds that being regenerated (saved) does not always result in deliverance from the demonic power. The question of deliverance from the demon often becomes an issue *after* salvation. The believer's newly acquired position in Christ becomes the basis of liberation from the evil spirit, not always the liberation itself.

Now, what is to be concluded when, for one reason or another, a true Christian falls prey to demon harassment or else manifests such evidences after a genuine conversion? That the person has "lost" his salvation? Certainly not! That he has never been saved? How can this be when he has shown all the fruits of salvation, often for many years?

The only solution to the problem is to face the facts of the case. This, we may be assured, will be in agreement with the Word of God correctly interpreted.

THE TESTIMONY OF EXPERIENCE

In an occult age, more and more Christians are being forced to face the full issue of the power that Satan and demons may hold over the life of a true believer who yields to temptation and sin. Thinking people realize that experience in pagan lands should not conflict with correct Bible doctrine taught in nonpagan lands. Many clearly see that theoretical and purely armchair theological interpretation that does not square with attested experience must be revised and brought into conformity with sound interpretation of the Word rather than with mere assumptions concerning what the Word teaches.

For many years the late chancellor of Wheaton College in Illinois, V. Raymond Edman, taught that a Christian under certain circumstances could be invaded by demonic powers. His firsthand experience with crude demonism, as a result of missionary labors in Ecuador in his earlier years, gave Dr. Edman an understanding of the subject sometimes not possessed by purely theoretical Bible interpreters.

In 1955, three years after the appearance of *Biblical Demonology*, Dr. Edman wrote me a letter stating his convictions on the subject. At the time I espoused the purely theoretical position, which did not square with the authenticated facts of experience.

Numerous other Christian leaders are beginning to comprehend the full extent to which demon power may affect the Christian. A Christian psychiatrist, Dr. Marion Nelson, declares that those who hold that a demon spirit cannot invade the same body as the Holy Spirit "must bear the burden of proving that it cannot happen, using Scripture properly interpreted and applied. This is difficult in the face of numerous reports of people who seem to be real Christians and who apparently suffer from demon possession."[3]

A Young Woman's Experience

The following testimony was given to me by a young woman while I was conducting a Bible conference in Dover, Delaware, in the fall of 1975. Because of its clarity and relevance to our topic, the story is given verbatim.

I did not grow up in a Christian home, so I really didn't know anything about salvation till I was thirteen years of age. At that time, through the kindness of my aunt and uncle, I went to a Christian ranch in Colora, Maryland. Almost the first time I heard the gospel I came under conviction. I knew I was a sinner and needed Christ as my Savior. I trusted Him and He saved me!

Oh how my life was changed! I just fell in love with Jesus Christ! He became my everything—my very life.

I returned home to an unchristian environment and took a stand for the Lord. But before even a year went by, I started to backslide, and some of my joy in the Lord vanished.

The following summer I went back to the ranch and there dedicated my life to Christ. But again, after a while I started to slip away from the Lord and hang around with the wrong people. Soon I was really in sin.

The kids I went with knew of my stand for Christ. But to be accepted by them I quit witnessing. Before long I found myself actually disowning Christ and making light of what I had testified to.

When I reached the age of fifteen, things began to go from bad to worse. The Beatles had become a world-famous singing group, and I honestly worshiped them. They took the place of God in my life. I would have literally sold myself to the devil to be with them.

Time after time the Holy Spirit corrected me. But I rejected His calling every time. At seventeen I married a boy in my school who was not a Christian. My life became miserable, and I started to drink. At times I became so intoxicated that I would pass out. Under the influence of liquor I would make a fool of myself before men and curse my husband in front of them. I got to a point where I just couldn't stand myself.

One evening as I sat alone in my living room, the Lord began to speak to me again. I was twenty-two years old. I asked God to forgive me for living in awful sin, and I rededicated my life to Christ.

Believe it or not, then began eighteen months of hell on earth for me. The very next morning I awoke terribly afraid. It seemed as if a great hand was around my heart, squeezing the very life out of me.

I began to study the Bible and pray and tried desperately to have fellowship with the Lord. I also started going to a Bible-preaching church. There I met some of the dearest Christian people in the world. Without their love and help I know I wouldn't be alive today, for in the following months I had a terrifying urge to take my own life.

I didn't know it then, but during my years of sin and turning my back on God, I had been invaded by a demon. As long as I lived in sin and drunkenness, and did what the demon wanted, he didn't bother me. But the moment I committed my life to Christ, the demon made my life one long torture session. I was constantly obsessed by terrible feelings of guilt. I know I must have run to the Lord a hundred times a day to ask forgiveness.

Awful fear gripped me. It is impossible for me to convey to any human being the horror of demonic fear. It hounded me when I attempted to read the Scripture or pray. It confused my mind when I tried to think about the things of God. I could take this torture for only about five or six days. Then you know what I would do—rather be compelled to do? I would get drunk!

Every time I got drunk or willfully sinned against the Lord, the pressure and the fear would stop! I did this two or three times a month. I would ask the Lord to forgive me. Then presto—the torture would start again. I yielded to God, cried out to Him, read every book I could lay hands on dealing with the victorious life. But the pressure, fear, and torment only got worse. Things got so bad, in fact, that I began planning to commit suicide.

The only thing that kept me from carrying out my plan was the thought that if I killed myself, my unsaved husband would go to hell. At this point my health gave way. I was on the verge of a mental and physical breakdown.

At this desperate juncture I cried to the Lord, asking Him to show me what this awful thing was that stood between us. Just as clearly as if someone had spoken to me, this thought came to me. *You have a demon!*

At this time I knew nothing about demons, except that I believed no believer, such as I was, could be possessed by one. I knew though that God had spoken. I became fearful, but the Lord wonderfully comforted me.

My first impulse was to tell my dear friend Shirley, who was a real student of the Bible. So I jumped in the car and drove to her house, telling her what had happened. She strongly disagreed with me, declaring that a Christian could *not* be demonized.

She suggested that we both go over to the parsonage and talk this over with Mrs. D_____, the pastor's wife. This we did, and I told her the story. She and the pastor were aware of the torment I had been experiencing.

Mrs. D_____ didn't say anything except that we should pray. The three of us knelt in front of her sofa. Mrs. D_____ laid her hand on my shoulder and began to pray softly. I started to call on the Lord. At that moment the pastor's wife quietly commanded the evil spirit to come out of me. When she did this, I began to feel a lurching inside me. I began to gag as though I were about to vomit. I couldn't catch my breath and had the sensation I was passing out, but actually it was the demon being expelled.

I was totally drained of strength and had to lie down and rest awhile. I felt as though the weight of two worlds had been taken off my shoulders and a new life was opening up for me.

The Lord has healed every wound in my heart and I know the abundant life He intends for His children to enjoy. I am balanced and secure. I'm in the hollow of His hand, and I'll never leave Him again. Praise God!

A DAUGHTER DELIVERED FROM DEMON POWER

A thrilling and moving story is told by Mrs. Frances Manuel, a Christian worker of Orlando, Florida. At the leading of the Lord, this dedicated servant of God was to become the adoptive mother of Beverly, the girl whose deliverance from demonic power is recounted here.[4]

When Frances Manuel first met Beverly, she was not really a child but almost as helpless as one, though in her late teens. Her face showed unmistakable evidences of fear and terrible inner turmoil. Her body displayed the scars of suffering and sin. Her whole being seemed to cry out in pitiable desperation, "Help! Please, somebody help me!"

The Lord had helped her. In fact, He had saved her just a few months before at a well-known Bible camp. But the perplexing thing was how *any* Christian could be in the distressing condition Beverly was in.

Part of Beverly's trouble was due to her having been addicted to heroin. When she was saved, however, she had been completely delivered from the habit. Even so, one doctor to whom she had been taken advised that unless she resumed taking heroin in small doses under his direction, she would die.

"I don't have to live" was her reply, "but I do have to stay away from dope! God saved me from that!"

In the early days of her association with Mrs. Manuel, Beverly had several strange seizures in which she lapsed into a prolonged coma. Asked how long she had been having these spells of unconsciousness, she said they had never been really bad until she had believed on Christ and was saved.

Mrs. Manuel had already concluded that Beverly's condition might be demonic. But how could this be? She had been taught and fully believed that a Christian could not be demonized. Yet, here before her was a case that apparently denied that and made her cry out to the Lord for wisdom to discern the truth.

It was at this time, as Beverly came out of her first coma and Mrs. Manuel witnessed her utter helplessness, that the Lord spoke to her about adopting Beverly as her daughter. It was a task she knew to be totally beyond her. But her faith surmounted all obstacles. After conflict, she yielded and entered into the assignment of becoming Beverly's new mother.

At that time Mrs. Manuel declared, "It was not Beverly's sin . . . nor the enormity of her need . . . that impressed me. It was the purity of her heart. . . . In her subconscious state she revealed a cleansed spirit and a heartfelt knowledge of the Lord Jesus . . . that moved me greatly."[5]

But the new mother-daughter relationship, instead of bringing victory, was the signal for war. Violent seizures— more violent and frequent than any the daughter had gone through up to that time faced them. In the deep comas, she would be hurled out of bed on her head with fearful force, as if by an intelligent being. In this state of unconsciousness she could not be awakened, although during these blackouts she occasionally spoke from her subconscious mind.

During such lapses into the demonized state, when the evil spirits took over, she would manifest superhuman strength—screaming, writhing, kicking, foaming at the mouth, clawing, and biting. Her eyes would glow with an ominous supernatural luster. Most despicably she would spit, usually the offense being aimed at her mother.

As she grew increasingly worse, at times she would make bestial sounds with her face taking on an animal-like expression. At times she would snarl and bark like a dog. At other times she would hiss like a serpent or laugh like a hyena.

Yet, with all these evidences, Mrs. Manuel still wondered if her adopted daughter suffered from true demon invasion. God answered her through a missionary from Brazil who had dealt with many cases of demonization on the field and who was thoroughly conversant with the phenomenon. When the missionary saw Beverly in a seizure, he immediately recognized her condition as not only a bona fide case of demon invasion, but one of unusual severity.

Uncertainty was now turned to assurance as far as Mrs. Manuel was concerned. The missionary, standing as her ally, with prayer confronted the demonic powers in Beverly with the bold command: "Demon, in the name of the Lord Jesus Christ, I demand you to give your name and come out of her."

Immediately eight demons gave their names in voices utterly distinct from Beverly's, though her vocal cords were employed. As the demons left, Beverly writhed, screamed, and nearly choked. Awakening out of the demonized state, she was left limp and exhausted. But perfect peace settled over her as she thanked and praised God for His mercy.

The missionary outlined the procedure to repulse further attacks and pointed out the strategy for an offensive to secure eventual complete deliverance. Further onslaughts came in the following months, always suddenly without warning. Beverly's mother, together with a small band of recruits who stood with her, would sing, read Scripture and pray, directly confronting and challenging the demons.

The fierce struggle with the demonic host indwelling Beverly lasted until October 14, 1956, the day she marked when her final deliverance took place. During this long war with intermittent terrible attacks, an incredible number of demons were expelled. Yet the struggle had been largely defensive, the sinister powers somehow taking the offensive and attacking at will and almost wearing out their opponents with exhaustion.

This undoubtedly was one of many reasons for the protracted conflict. There were obvious other reasons. God was showing Beverly and all concerned the exceeding heinousness and harmfulness of sin as well as His grace and holiness. If quick victory had been granted, Beverly might have been tempted to give ground for reinvasion of the demon hordes.

But above all, God, who had called Mrs. Manuel to this ministry by entrusting to her a demon-controlled daughter, was teaching His obedient servant the lessons she had to learn to help later in the release of others, enchained as Beverly was by the powers of Satan.

Then, too, Mrs. Manuel and her helpers needed to discover that they had foolishly allowed the powers of darkness to take the initiative to attack at their will to wear them down and delay, if not rule out, complete victory altogether. When God's servants saw their mistake and boldly seized the offensive, complete victory was promptly realized.

At the last memorable session, when the final demons made their exit, Beverly writhed, groaned, and coughed in indescribable agony. Suddenly there was a complete lull. There she lay, fully conscious, perfectly relaxed. Looking up at her mother and smiling serenely, she said faintly, *"Mother, they're all gone!"* Totally exhausted, she fell into a deep and restful sleep.

At last the Lord's child, taken captive by the powers of darkness, was free—free indeed! "If the Son therefore shall make you free, ye shall be free indeed" (John 8:36).

On two occasions afterward, Beverly had encounter with the demon army that had invaded and possessed her. They returned to demand reentrance. But no longer could they enter at will. It required Beverly's consent. This, of course, she steadfastly refused. Praise God! These evil spirits have long since ceased their wicked demands. Beverly was perfectly delivered to live a normal happy Christian life, later assuming the role of a devoted Christian wife and mother.

6

WHAT PROTECTION DO BELIEVERS HAVE AGAINST DEMONS?

To hear many believers speak today about the powers of darkness, one would conclude that becoming a Christian automatically shields a person, if not from satanic and demonic attack, then certainly from demonic invasion and despoilment. But if Satan and demons can and do attack, which hardly any instructed and experienced Christian can deny, the question must be squarely faced: What happens if satanic and demonic onslaughts are not resisted? Will the powers of evil merely leave the believer alone simply because he is in Christ?

A still more pressing problem remains. What happens if not only an attack is not countered but the fortress of the believer's position in Christ is unguarded and the doors left wide open by flagrant disobedience and willful, persistent sin?

Careful facing of the issues involved in the light of the testimony of the Word reveals that the experience of salvation furnishes no *magical* protection against Satan and demons. Salvation, however, does provide *miraculous* protection (God working supernaturally). And what a difference there is between the two.

This miraculous protection is the result of appropriating the power of God. The Holy Spirit who indwells the believer is the power of God. He is "greater" than Satan and his hosts who are "in the world" (1 John 4:4), and he effects victory in the believer on the basis of the believer's faith in what he is in Christ. Believers who do not know what they are in Christ and so do not count on that position do not enjoy automatic protection from demonic despoilment and intrusion.

THE EXTENT OF THE CHRISTIAN'S PROTECTION

In considering how far Satan and demons can go in enslaving a Christian, it is necessary, as noted throughout this book, to distinguish carefully between the believer's position before God and his experience of that position. The former is that sphere in which God views the believer as taken out of the realm of sin and condemnation in Adam (Romans 5:12-20) and placed eternally and unforfeitably in the realm of righteousness and justification in Christ (Romans 6:1-12).

Satan and demon powers can never alter this unchangeable placement. In Christ the believer is eternally secure and assured a glorified body and heaven as his destiny. Satan and demons, although powerless to change the believer's position, can destroy the believer's experience of that position for a time. In fact, the believer's position in Christ makes the Christian a target of demonic malignity.

Satan and his minions waste no time bemoaning what they cannot do. They bend every effort to do what they can do, namely, rob the believer of the enjoyment of his glorious position before God. That is why the apostle Paul in his epistles so fully and magnificently sets forth the believer's position in Christ (Romans 6:1-10; Ephesians 1:3-21) and demonstrates that it is the knowledge of and faith in that position (Romans 6:11) that is the basis of victory over sin and constitutes the source of the power that puts to flight the powers of darkness.

For this reason, demonic principalities and powers are included in the list of what shall not be able to separate us from the love of God manifested in our salvation through Christ Jesus—our Lord (Romans 8:38-39). Why? In his position in Christ, the believer is exalted "far above all principality, and power," as joined to the risen glorified Lord in heaven, who is so exalted (Ephesians 1:21).

In Christ, the believer is regenerated (John 3:3, 5), justified (Romans 5:1), baptized by the Spirit into union with His Lord (1 Corinthians 12:13; Romans 6:3-4), indwelt by the Spirit forever (1 Corinthians 6:19-20), sealed by the Spirit unto the day of redemption (Ephesians 4:30), and positionally filled with the Spirit (Colossians 2:9-10). All these mighty undertakings guarantee that those whom Christ has redeemed can never be taken away from Christ by Satan and demons.

Accordingly, Scripture clearly reveals that the believer is absolutely protected from Satan and demons in his *position* before God in Christ by virtue of the "so great salvation" he enjoys (Hebrews 2:3). However, as far as his *experience* is concerned, protection against demonic attack is *only in proportion* to what the believer *knows and believes* to be his position, in this way making it realizable in his experience (Romans 6:11). This is simply saying that victory over Satan and demons, like victory over the world and sin itself, is by faith—that is, by believing we are what we are in Christ and resting in what Christ has done in redeeming us (1 John 5:4).

The Bible pointedly teaches that the believer has been set free from sin (Romans 6:6-7, 18). But if he fails to reckon himself (by faith count himself) dead to sin and alive to God in his position of union with Christ (Romans 6:11-13; Galatians 5:16), he will soon give place to sin in his life. In the same way, while he has been delivered from the powers of darkness, it is only as he counts on his position in Christ and employs the resources of that position in resisting the enemy that the defeated foe will flee from him (James 4:7; Ephesians 6:10-18).

It may then be said that the Christian's protection in an absolute sense is limited to his position in Christ. That position is an impregnable fortress, which all the hosts of hell cannot break through. God creates that fortress and guards its inviolability by the redemptive work of His Son and the unchangeable truth of His Word.

But the Christian's protection, as far as the *experience* of his position is concerned, is always relative, never absolute. It is an impregnable fortress only as its impregnable defenses are reckoned upon and put to use. Similarly, in his position before God in Christ, the believer is a fully panoplied soldier against whom Satan and demons are powerless. But in his experience, Satan and demons can and will penetrate that armor unless the Christian warrior uses every part of it in resisting the enemy's attack (Ephesians 6:10-18).

How Far Can Demons Go?

As mentioned previously, a demon may gain control of the body of a Christian as a squatter when the indwelling Holy Spirit is seriously grieved by sin or quenched by rank disobedience or open rebellion against God's will. Certainly by permitting heinous sin or indulging in occultism or occult religion or yielding to some other transgression, a believer limits the protection that is his in Christ.

The situation may be compared to a man who owns a house. If he completely controls it and occupies it, no one, of course, can move in without his approval. But if he does not occupy all the rooms and is lax concerning who visits and how long they stay, he may soon find himself with an illegal dweller or two who may prove very difficult to get rid of. In fact, it may be impossible to expel them except by physical force or recourse to the law.

Jesus spoke of an evil spirit who had gone out of a man. When the demon desired to return to his habitation, he did so because he found it "empty" (not filled with the Spirit), "swept" (clean of dirt), and "garnished" (adorned with moral refinements). Not only was the demon able to return himself, but he took with him "seven other spirits more wicked than himself" (Matthew 12:43-45).

The lesson to be learned from Jesus' illustration is that not only grievous sins of the *flesh* open the door to demon invasion. Sins of the *spirit*, notably pride and self-righteousness, do the same.

It is quite obvious that a Christian indwelt by the Holy Spirit may not necessarily be controlled by Him. If the believer is not controlled by the Spirit, he will be dominated by the flesh. The works of the flesh (Galatians 5:19-21) show a close affinity with the powers of darkness. Satan and demons operate through the flesh to the degree that it is not reckoned dead, and to that degree they gain control of the life through the old nature (cf. Ephesians 2:2).

How far can demons go if the old nature is coddled? They will go just as far as the carnal Christian allows them to go. The satanic strategy has always been to go just as far as he can in any life, whether saved or unsaved. The degree to which the old nature is indulged, in the life of either the unsaved or the saved, furnishes the degree to which Satan and demonic forces may control the life.

Dare we be so naive as to believe that demonic powers will not press their claims to the limit in any life? How much more in the case of the child of God! Failing to count on what he is in Christ, neglecting to use his resources in warfare, and, above all, opening the door to the enemy by serious and persistent sin, does the believer dare to presume that he will not be attacked, defeated, oppressed, or even invaded by the enemy?

Turned Over to Satan

Scripture clearly teaches that believers who sin shamelessly and scandalously may be delivered over to Satan "for the destruction of the flesh" (1 Corinthians 5:5). This means the sinning saint, as the ultimate in divine chastening, is turned over to Satan and demonic power to inflict physical death upon him. Satan has "the power of death" (Hebrews 2:14). He can kill the body of a seriously sinning saint who, by scandalous transgression, exposes himself to his power in this regard.

Jesus warned, "Fear not them which kill the body, but are not able to kill the soul" (Matthew 10:28). He was referring to wicked demon-driven men who, under the control of Satan and his hosts, have "the power of [physical] death" to murder people (Hebrews 2:14). At the same time our Lord indicated the limit of Satan's power. The evil one can kill the body but not the soul. He can inflict physical death if the believer exposes himself to it by flagrant sin, but he can never inflict spiritual death upon one who possesses spiritual life. Only God has the power to "destroy both soul and body in hell" (Matthew 10:28).[1] This He must do in the case of all who reject His salvation through Christ.

The sinning believer was to be turned over to Satan because of his shameless immorality. God's purpose was not that he might go to hell, but quite the opposite—that his "spirit may be saved in the day of the Lord Jesus" (1 Corinthians 5:5). He was to be subjected to the ultimate in the divine chastening—premature physical death—as a consequence of being turned over to Satan's power for the severest form of the Father's disciplinary dealing with His erring children.

Similarly, other sinning saints at Corinth had been afflicted with physical weakness, sickness, and premature physical death (1 Corinthians 11:30-32). They evidently had been turned over to Satan and demonic powers for the destruction of the flesh, not to be condemned with the world, but the very opposite, that they might "*not* be condemned with the world" (v. 32).

The apostle John also refers to this "sin unto [physical] death" (1 John 5:16*b*). It is not to be prayed for because it entails disciplinary action that the Father Himself cannot withhold due to the gravity of the sin committed. "There is a sin unto death: I do not say that he shall pray for it" (1 John 5:16*b*).

Now the question that arises is this: If being turned over to Satan has its ultimate degree realized in premature physical death, with physical weakness and sickness as intermediate stages, it is difficult to imagine how various stages of demonic influence and various degrees of demonization can be excluded.

Since *some* sicknesses are not the result of purely natural causes but are demonic in origin and, in the case of sinning saints, divinely disciplinary in purpose, deliverance over to Satan seems to involve various stages of demonic operation. Luke the physician speaks of "certain women-... healed of evil spirits and infirmities" (physical sicknesses). He specifically mentions Mary Magdalene, "out of whom went seven demons" (Luke 8:2).

There seems to be the possibility that God will allow a believer to undergo a period of demonic invasion to cure him of pride, arrogance, or some other sin that violates his Christian testimony and brings reproach upon the Lord's name and Christ's salvation.[2]

It is even possible for an obedient Spirit-led believer by God's design to experience a protracted period of demon activity as a preparation for a ministry of deliverance.

During a teaching ministry in Brazil in the spring of 1976, I came in contact with such a believer. The Lord had permitted her to pass through two years of severe demonic struggle. Then He completely set her free to enter her present widely used counseling ministry with the occultly oppressed.

OPERATION OF THE LAWS OF THE SPIRIT WORLD

God is a God of law and order. When He created the earth and man upon the earth, He established certain natural physical laws for the operation of an orderly universe. God does not set aside these laws. When He performs a miracle,

He transcends them, rather than sets them aside, by the operation of the higher laws of the spiritual realm.

For example, the law of gravity operates rigidly. Satan tempted our Lord to ignore it. Casting Himself down from the pinnacle of the Temple would not have been trusting God and His Word but, instead, tempting God and dishonoring His Word (Matthew 4:5-7). Disaster alone can result if we thus defy God's order. God's physical laws operate just as rigidly upon the Christian as the non-Christian.

God has established law and order in the spiritual realm as in the natural sphere. These laws that govern the angels and demons and Satan himself are just as unbending as those that govern man in the natural realm. For reasons not fully revealed, God has permitted the powers of darkness a circumscribed sphere of activity in the fallen race, both in unsaved humanity as well as among the saved.

When the believer ventures into the supernatural realm, the laws that regulate that realm operate upon him just as inflexibly as the laws of the natural realm in which he normally moves.[3] He expects to get violently ill or die if he swallows poison. So if he gluts his mind with obscene thoughts and pollutes his spiritual life with the occult, he may expect to land in immorality and error and be plundered by Satan and demons. When the believer enters forbidden areas, he not only limits the protection that is his in Christ but also opens the door and gives the enemy entrance. He must bear in mind that, as a believer, he is a special target for demonic powers who will not rest until they have reduced him to the lowest enslavement possible.

DEMONS AND THE THREEFOLD NATURE OF MAN

Man is revealed to be a tripartite creature composed of spirit, soul, and body (1 Thessalonians 5:23). The highest part of man, the spirit, is that which possesses self-consciousness and "knows" (1 Corinthians 2:11; NASB). The regenerated spirit "knows" God and enjoys fellowship with

Him (Job 32:8; cf. Proverbs 20:27), because the regenerated spirit is the particular abode of the Holy Spirit through whom the believer knows "the things of God" (1 Corinthians 2:ll-l2).

The new nature bestowed at regeneration constitutes the sphere in which the Holy Spirit works in the believer through his regenerated human spirit. The powers of darkness cannot invade or indwell that holy sanctum. This seems obvious because God's "seed" (the new nature) remains in the believer alongside the old nature. God's child, therefore, cannot practice sin as a habit (1 John 3:9). If he does, he demonstrates himself, says John, to be a member of the devil's family and not of God's family (1 John 3:8, 10).

However, through crass indulgence of the old nature, demon powers can influence the believer through his *body* and *soul.* In cases where the sin is of such a character that it goes beyond the old nature, the demon may invade and cause upheaval and chaos in the believer through his body and soul. In this case, the child of God displays a kind of split personality. First he speaks and acts through the Spirit, but then under the influence of the demon power when it is in control.

But it is my conviction that the new *nature* and the Spirit-indwelt human *spirit* cannot be invaded by demonic powers since the new (regenerated) man is a partaker of the divine nature and life (Colossians 3:3-4; 2 Peter 1:4) in which Satan and demons can have no part.

In the case of the unsaved, Satan and demons *can* dominate and enslave the entire personality—body, soul, and spirit. Deliverance, moreover, is impossible apart from salvation. Position in Christ is the ground of all deliverance from sin and the powers of darkness that have no rightful place in the believer.

A MISSIONARY FACES A DEMONIZED BELIEVER

The following letter deals with the question of whether or not a believer can be demonized. It was written on August

21, 1956 by a missionary working among the Ohontal Indians of Mexico to the late Dr. James F. Rand, then librarian of Dallas Theological Seminary.

DEAR DR. RAND:

Today in reading your Periodical Review of the July, 1956 issue of your Seminary quarterly, *Bibliotheca Sacra,* I was very much interested in your appraisal of the article in the current *Moody Monthly* by William Young, entitled, "Demons Today?" What interested me most of all was your statement that you do not believe that believers can be possessed by demons.

My wife and I, graduates of Wheaton College and Moody Bible Institute respectively, are missionaries laboring among the natives of Tabasco. About seven years ago we had an experience among our converts which makes us feel assured that believers can be demon-possessed [demonized]. Previous to this instance, we both were persuaded that a believer could not be demon-possessed [demonized].

This case has to do with a young man, an Indian, who we both are assured is saved. Before this experience with this young Indian, we had felt demon opposition in our home— hearing footsteps on the floor, but seeing nothing in a direct beam of light, witnessing a mattress bouncing up and down with nothing on it.

This young man began to manifest demonic symptoms by a sickness that showed no physical cause at all. A little while later I was called late one night. He had jumped into the well! After pulling him out, and then talking and praying with him and his family for an hour, I came to the conclusion that his trouble was demonic.

When I finally left the house after another hour of counseling and praying, *a demon followed me out!* It was the experience of a real presence, evil, terrifying, yet hard to explain. I could literally sense that being trying to gain entrance to my life. My desire was to start in a headlong run. But, praise God, I didn't run. I stood my ground and prayed. For two or three days a constant battle raged, before the evil spirit quit and left me.

Then the young man, whose name was Fernando, got worse again. I went to see him and talked very frankly with him about his salvation. With tears he assured me that he was saved, but that he would go empty-handed into the Lord's presence, because he had little faith. Moreover, he was certain that he was going to die, because he had been so weak spiritually. He complained also that at times he saw spectres around the room.

Two days later he had another attack. I and five other men went to see him. Standing at the head of his bed, I saw him suddenly looking wildly at something across the room and he cried out, "Why have you come to torment me?"

In an instant his voice changed (the demon taking over) and glaringly he turned to us, yelling loudly, "Who are you? I am stronger than all of you!"

With that he began to scream, curse, kick, and swing his arms violently. His strength was such that the six of us could not hold him down. Fortunately help soon arrived. At the end of two hours he quieted down somewhat, but it had taken eight to ten men at a time to control him. After two hours seventeen strong young men were worn out, yet he was still as strong as ever.

These outbursts would usually come at night. As a rule he slept all morning, and in the afternoon was more or less normal. At these times he would talk and act quite sanely. He was very sure he was going to die as a chastening from the Lord, but equally certain he was saved.

Before the demon took control, he generally knew it and would say, "It is coming. Grab me!"

During these attacks, his voice would change completely (the demon talking through him). Even his face would be altered completely. Often he would under seizure attempt to injure himself.

On several occasions he told the time of the day exactly, despite the fact that I had the only watch in the crowd. He would call himself prince of power of this or that and suddenly lapse into speaking in a foreign tongue.

Finally one night, after a violent attack, he quieted down and became unconscious. A doctor was called, but said there was nothing he could do. I went home and got my folding ruler to measure the body to make a casket at the request of the young man's father, a firm Christian.

Meanwhile when his pulse beat became so weak that I could only get it at the jugular vein and the patient began to get cold, the end seemed very near.

While he was unconscious, I heard him speaking as though to the Lord—very softly and reverently. Suddenly he opened his eyes, sat up, and spoke to me. He declared the Lord had given him "an hour." He wanted to see my wife (we had both often counseled with him) and all the members of his family.

When we were all assembled, his plea to us was, "Fear and serve the Lord. Take note of what happened to me."

At the end of the hour I expected him to die. When it passed, I asked him about it.

He appeared puzzled, saying, "The Lord didn't say if it was an hour by a watch or what. I don't know!"

He was sure, however, that he had been told to testify for the Lord. This he did consistently and several came to know the Lord, and every one of these has remained true to the Lord to this day. . . .

With this the spiritual life of the congregation began its upsurge. Three neighboring churches also experienced growth and blessing as a result of this incident.

Fernando continued with a constant, sincere testimony, as well as with a warning to others to consider what had happened to him. As a result a number of young people dedicated their lives to the Lord, and three years later several came to study in our Bible Institute. . . .

From all we have witness to, my wife and I both feel sure that Fernando is saved, "yet so as by fire" (1 Corinthians 3:15), that and no more. We are also both certain that he is demonized. To us it is a very sobering fact, and Fernando's case has had a very sobering effect upon more than one weak believer in our locality.

Our inescapable conclusions regarding this instance cross your point theologically. Yet I feel sure we have seen cases of true believers who were demon-possessed [demonized]. It has always been a problem theologically, something I cannot explain, except that nowhere does the Scripture specifically state that a believer cannot be demon-possessed [demonized]. It rather implies that, under certain conditions, he can.

A BELIEVER DECEIVED BY SEDUCING SPIRITS

Many earnest, sincere children of God do not realize the peril they incur when they seek for a physical and emotional experience not authenticated by the Word of God. They do not know that in persistently following such a course they open themselves to invasion by "deceitful [seducing] spirits" and to falling prey to "doctrines of demons" (1 Timothy 4:1; NASB).

A sad illustration came to me recently from the wife of a Baptist minister in Kansas. She wrote me thanking me for my book *Demons in the World Today.* She said, "It has been a source of help to me in getting out of one of Satan's snares." In telling me of the terrible bondage to demon powers she fell under, she began by describing her salvation at the age of ten. This is her testimony of her subsequent Christian life:

> Many times during the next twenty years a great hunger came to my soul to know the Lord better. Not being a student of the Word, I did not really understand the simplicity of God's teaching to be filled with the Spirit and walk in the Spirit.
>
> In 1967 a friend gave me a book about speaking in tongues. My spiritual life was at a low ebb, and I was intensely seeking after God. I knew I was saved, but there seemed to be an emptiness in my soul.
>
> After reading this book, I began to believe that the experience of tongues was necessary to fill the spiritual void. For six years I asked for the experience.
>
> During 1973 I became ill. The desire for a closer fellowship with the Lord and to have the power of God upon my life became more intense than ever before. I read several books

on tongues . . . and I began seeking out people who had this experience.

My husband, a Baptist minister and a student of the Word, would explain the Scripture teaching on this subject, but my mind was made up that tongues were the ultimate and only reliable evidence of being Spirit-filled.

I contacted a charismatic Baptist minister and received the laying on of hands, which brought a most ecstatic experience . . . undoubtedly supernatural. I had never experienced such a wonderful feeling—too different to be merely psychological. I felt certain no one had ever been so happy, contented, and filled with joy.

Tongues did not come to me with the laying on of hands, but I kept asking for them. Two months later they came, accompanied with unusual happenings.

Each day was a new and wonderful experience. Prayers were answered, miraculously, and always in the name of Jesus. One of the greatest deceits is the "other Jesus spirits," who do not confess Jesus Christ as Savior and Lord (1 John 4:2; 2 Corinthians 11:4).

At that time no one could have made me believe that Satan could produce these happenings, although the Word of God warns that he is "prince of the power of the air" (Ephesians 2:2).

The week that tongues came to me, strange happenings occurred inside my body. My will had no control over the happenings, and I was doing nothing to produce them.

Some of the manifestations were lewd and my mind was greatly disturbed, since they always came after the tongues, which I supposed were produced by the Holy Spirit.

The tongues were new and exciting, and I used them frequently at first. I knew the physical happenings were demonic, but I thought Satan was trying to defeat the wonderful experience of the Holy Spirit.

I was filled with glory over the tongues, but at the same time, suffered agony over the constant evil that prevailed. I returned to my charismatic friends time after time for help. Each time there was the laying on of hands and the command for Satan to leave me alone.

Although the physical manifestations never left me, for several days I would have relief from the mental oppression.

I asked for more tongues, going deeper into the experience, trying to get away from Satan. When the glory of the "high" was over after each tongues experience, the presence of evil was more prominent.

Many times it seemed the entire room was filled with evil.

Several months after receiving the tongues experience and alternating from day to day between glory and misery, a still, small voice spoke definitely to me, saying that the tongues were a form of Satan worship. Being certain that this was the work of the Holy Spirit, I was horrified, although the suspicion had existed for some time.

Being increasingly certain that I was being controlled by Satan, I determined to resist him. Torment beyond description followed. Voices would speak to me about the most hideous things imaginable.

Horrible suspicions about my husband and dear Christian friends took hold of me. Terrifying dreams and nightmares occurred. Voices said that I should die because I was corrupt, and God would never use me now.

Sometimes becoming desperate with fear of losing my sanity and life, I would yield to the tongues which were welling up within me. Great relief followed, until I refused them expression again.

Many times I called upon the Lord and claimed the blood of Christ. But each time I would be thrown to the floor in agony. Fourteen months after receiving the tongues, I was ready to take my life.

As a final plea for help, I called a very dear Baptist minister-friend, who knew something of these Satanic workings among God's people. He worked and prayed with my husband and me about three months. Other ministers prayed with us, sometimes for several hours at a time.

During this time we saw the power of the resurrected Christ demonstrated against the foe in a spectacular way.

Although I had lent myself through ignorance to the influence of the evil powers of Satan, the Lord in love continued to draw me out of the snare of the enemy.

It has been a long journey back from the realm of darkness into which I had gone so deeply, but the grace of the Lord Jesus Christ has been sufficient to meet every need.

This is not a conviction or accusation of others who speak with tongues. I am only testifying of what is true in my personal experience as a result of my mind having been corrupted from the simplicity that is in Christ (2 Corinthians 11:3).

I have many friends and loved ones in the Pentecostal-Charismatic movement whose desire is to serve the Lord Jesus Christ. Many of them preach the true Gospel of Salvation. Some of these became very dear to me during the times of great stress and had a sincere desire to help and encourage me.

I am indebted to a good friend, who is a teacher and counselor with wide experience in dealing with the demonically oppressed, for the following clinical case.

The Day of Prayer, 1975, and the day that followed, were days of great confrontation with demons in the body of Mrs. H. M., a fine Christian wife and mother. She had called us for help. Dr. F. D. had met with her for three hours the day before the Day of Prayer. He realized from that experience that there would be a great battle against the demons. He contacted me, and we went with Mrs. H. M. in his office. She insisted that we move to a larger room because she felt that there would be violent actions by the demons in her. We agreed to follow her advice.

Dr. F. D. shared with me his diagnosis and convictions concerning the case. She would fill in the information as we questioned her further. As I began to probe with questions, the evil spirit surfaced and spoke to us while Mrs. H. M. was knocked out. The battle was on! It raged five hours except for an hour of lunch. The demon voice that spoke out of her was rough and deep. Her eyes during the fierce struggle literally crossed and rolled around in their sockets. Her face was swollen to about twice the normal size. Her hands looked like bird claws. The demons would cause her body to rise up and start menacingly toward us.

We would say in a Spirit-filled seemingly calm voice, "Sit down, leave her eyes alone, leave her hands alone." Either of us, sometimes both of us, would demand in the name of the Lord Jesus Christ, the demon's name, ground, and reason for being in her body. It would reluctantly tell us.

We would call her back to consciousness, advise her to renounce the demons and claim victory in Christ. We would encourage her to tell the demons to leave, which they did. Sometimes very quickly, sometimes after a long confrontation, Mrs. H. M. was able to sense the leaving of the particular group of demons.

We continued this strategy over and over until all but one demon had left the battlefield. He refused to leave. We realized that she was weary and needed a rest. We were not able to bind the demon until after lunch.

After lunch we battled furiously for another hour. Then we agreed that we would give the demon a time limit to come out. After a short ten-minute raging battle, with the demon calling for Satan to send help while we were praying to God to send angels to stop Satan, the evil spirit came out. All of us felt the peace that seemed to fill the room. How we praised God for seeing Him victorious over Satan and his demons.

The next day she came for added help and more demons left her. Since that day we have used her in giving her testimony, and she is doing fine. Both Dr. F. D. and I agreed that it was the most fearful battle we had ever faced.

During the battle Mrs. H. M. was not aware of what was going on except for a few after effects of the terrible conduct. She shared with us how her wrists and fingers ached because of the demons using her hands and fingers to reach toward us. Her husband, who did not believe that demons could invade or control a Christian, wept as he saw his wife in a helpless demonized condition. He has been able to come to her aid when these evil powers have tried to come back to reinvade her. God is now using her to help others.

7

WHAT DO THE SCRIPTURES SAY?

The confusion and uncertainty in the minds of many believers concerning whether it is possible for a believer to be demonized are due to a large extent to misinterpretation of Scripture evidence.

It is a common practice today to construe certain passages of the Word of God relating to the question under discussion in such a way as to have an apparent smack of orthodoxy but to be out of line with plain, authenticated experience.

Experience, of course, is never to be the real test of spiritual truth. Revealed truth itself furnishes the basic and only valid criterion. Yet it follows that revealed truth is never at variance with genuine experience. When a clash occurs, the culprit is the interpretation of the truth or the alleged experience, not the truth itself.

DEMON INVASION AND DEMON POSSESSION

Both demon invasion and so-called "demon possession" are, as already noted, more accurately defined biblically as "demonization" (Gk. *daimonizomai,* meaning "being demonized," i.e., "under the control of one or more demons"; see Matthew 4:24; Mark 1:32; Luke 8:31*b*). Another Greek expression means "to have a demon" *(echei daimonion*; see Luke 7:33; John 7:20).

Hence, the Scriptures speak of people "being demonized" or "having a demon or demons." While popular terminology speaks of "demon possession," the more scripturally accurate designation is "demonization (being demonized) as the result of control by one or more demons."

It is evident, then, that *all* demonic invasion is demonization of whatever degree of mildness or severity. To call it "demon possession" rather than demonization is biblically permissible, but *only* insofar as the usage does *not* attempt to differentiate it from demonization in general or limit it to some cases (the milder forms) rather than all cases (including the more severe forms).

Much of the opposition to the possibility that demons can invade and control a believer stems from the failure to see that *all* invasion, however mild it may be, constitutes demonization (being demonized). Unfortunately, the term "demon possession" has been commonly used, not to refer correctly to *all* cases of demon invasion, but incorrectly to refer *only* to the basest and most enslaving forms, such as those represented by the demoniac of Gadara (Mark 5:1-20).

While cases of severe demonization are indeed a far cry from very mild forms, they are nevertheless mere variations in degree of the same supernatural phenomenon. Both involve demonic invasion and both involve a degree of satanic control. In one case the oppression is relatively light. In the other case the powers of darkness hold their victim in a viselike grip, possessing him as in the dark days of human slavery when a slave was chattel and could be abused freely by an unscrupulous master.

Extreme demonization is possible only where ignorance and sin have given the powers of darkness access to human personality through centuries of entrenched paganism (cf. 1 Corinthians 10:20-21). Yet, on mission fields where believers have been saved out of such devil control, converts must keep separate from demon-energized paganism or they will again be entrapped in the abysmal slavery out of which Christ rescued them (1 Corinthians 10:22).

In civilized lands where Christianity and cultural advance have been a beneficent influence for centuries, few Christians are victimized by demonization in its baser forms. But the situation is quite different in the case of milder forms. To this lesser degree of demonization, it is feared, in an age of spreading occultism and moral laxity, more and more believers are becoming invaded by demon powers and are being afflicted with physical, mental, emotional, and moral problems that unmistakably go beyond natural infirmities and disabilities or the normal struggle between the flesh and the spirit.

While I was writing this chapter my telephone rang. On the line was a Christian woman who had been a believer for five years, in loving fellowship with Christ and dutiful service to God. Suddenly, four months previously, an evil spirit for some reason entered her life, tormenting her with doubts about her salvation, periodically controlling her and causing her to rebel against God, and filling her mind and lips with blasphemy. When she talked with me by phone, she was momentarily free of the evil, invading personality and weepingly protested her love and devotion to the Lord Jesus.

Like many other Christians, this woman found her personality split. In her normal state controlled by the Holy Spirit, she humbly and willingly served the Lord. In the demonized state, when an evil spirit asserted authority, she was a totally different individual—rebellious, blasphemous, and utterly profane.

SCRIPTURE INTIMATIONS

Scripture nowhere expressly declares that a believer may not be invaded by demon power. On the other hand, God's Word contains intimations that the powers of darkness may invade the believer under certain conditions.

Saul was a believer (1 Samuel 10:9). God gave him "another heart." Early in life he enjoyed the anointing of God's Spirit (1 Samuel 10-12). Through sin and disobedience he forfeited God's manifested presence and became invaded by a demon spirit (1 Samuel 16:14). It is called "an evil spirit from the Lord" (1 Samuel 16:14; cf. v. 23) because it was permitted by God as a chastening upon His disobedient child. To argue that Saul was not a believer is to argue that the Spirit of God may anoint an unbeliever (1 Samuel 10:1, 10) and that God would appoint an unbeliever over His inheritance.

The precise reason King Saul was invaded by a demon is not indicated. It seems, however, that it was because of his spirit of stubborn rebellion against God. Samuel declared, "Rebellion is as the sin of witchcraft" (1 Samuel 15:23), and in the very next chapter (1 Samuel 16:14, 23) Saul is invaded by a demon.

King Ahab and Jehoshaphat, when they proposed to fight against the Syrians, inquired of the Lord by gathering 400 prophets (1 Kings 22:6). It is hard to imagine that Micaiah was the only true believer in the Lord among this large company, because they all *inquired of the Lord,* not Baal. Yet all, except Micaiah, yielding to pressure from wicked Ahab, received a spirit of deception and came under demon control (1 Kings 22:19-22; cf. 1 John 4:1).

Evidently at least some of the false prophets of Israel were regenerated and initially God-called (Deuteronomy 13:1-5; Jeremiah 23:21-22). Yet, under fierce persecution, they gave in to compromise and sin and certainly were invaded by demon powers to attempt to turn the Lord's people away from God to idols. Zechariah connects "the prophets" with "the unclean spirit" (demonic powers energizing the false prognosticators; see Zechariah 13:2; cf. Jeremiah 23:14-15).

Luke the physician diagnosed the strange physical disability of a certain believer as demonic. The woman in question had a disorder of the spine and for eighteen years had been bent double. She is said to have been bound by "a spirit of infirmity," that is, a demon caused her problem. Her case was the result of Satan binding her. Apparently she was a regenerated believer, "a daughter of Abraham" (Luke 13:10-16; cf. Romans 4:11, 16; Galatians 3:7) and not merely a lineal descendant of Abraham. Jesus healed her by delivering her from the demon that was causing her physical difficulty (cf. Luke 7:21). Mary Magdalene was healed when seven demons went out of her, possibly after she had been a believer for some time (Luke 8:2).

Cases such as this, which baffle doctors, surgeons, and psychiatrists, occur daily among Christians and frequently among missionaries and other Christian workers. The difficulty, whether physical, emotional, mental, or spiritual, is *purely* demonic. When the demon (or demons) is cast out, the problem vanishes.

Demons attack the mind to gain a foothold in the lives of people. Satan blinds the minds of the unsaved to keep them away from the light of the gospel (2 Corinthians 4:3-4). To resist demon influence, a Christian must guard against what he reads and what sort of television he permits himself to view or what radio programs he listens to. If he is not wary, demon influence may merge into demon obsession. If not curbed, demon invasion (demonization) may ultimately eventuate.

The apostle warned his converts of the peril of satanic activity to corrupt the believer's mind to turn him away "from the simplicity that is in Christ" (2 Corinthians 11:3). Satan and demonic spirits accomplish this in the same subtle manner in which they deceived Eve at the beginning. For this reason the believer's mental life must be constantly renewed by dedication to God's Word and will (Romans 12:2; Ephesians 4.17-18, 22-23).

The importance of guarding the thought life against demonic intrusion is again stressed by the apostle. He refers to the believer's spiritual "weapons" that are "mighty through

God to the pulling down of strongholds," in which the powers of darkness lodge themselves in the mind. This warfare results in the "casting down of imaginations, and every high thing that exalteth itself against the knowledge of God, and bringing into captivity every thought to the obedience of Christ" (2 Corinthians 10:4-5).

The imaginations and speculations that demons build in the mind become the fortresses in which they entrench themselves and from which they attack (2 Corinthians 11:3-4). To drive out the demon—"another spirit" (2 Corinthians 11:4)—these fortresses must be destroyed. Demons hang on tenaciously and cannot be dislodged until the ideas and heresies they have engendered in the mind are eradicated.

The apostle John warns the "beloved" people of God not to believe every spirit but to put the spirits to the test because many false prophets are energized by evil spirits that fill their minds with error and false doctrine and thus enslave them (1 John 4:1).

"In the latter times," the Spirit declares, "some shall depart from the faith" (1 Timothy 4:1). These must be believers who turn and become heretics, for only such could leave true Christianity. The result is that they get involved with "seducing [wandering] spirits" and land in "doctrines of devils [demons]," denoting teachings instigated by demons (v. 1). Departure from the faith does not necessarily mean defection from Christ, although apostates are no more excluded from this passage than are heretics. Rather, it suggests departure from revealed truth. This doctrinal deterioration allows for the various stages of contact with the powers of darkness in demonization, depending on the severity of doctrinal lapse and the type of cult in which the victim is ensnared. Demon control is not unknown among believers who give themselves wholly to the demonic doctrines taught by the cults. Witness the blindness and insulation against the truth that result.

Activity in the realm of religion in spawning and propagating error is the chief occupation of Satan and demons, and it constitutes their most successful role (1 Timothy 4:1-2; 1 John 4:1-6). While demonic influence is doubtless more common in this sphere, demonic invasion is not excluded (2 Corinthians 11:4).

SCRIPTURE DECLARATIONS

Besides intimations that demons may invade and control a Christian, the Bible contains declarations that suggest the possibility that such a thing may occur. Ignorance or wishful thinking on this question exposes believers to the peril of plunder by the powers of darkness.

Paul testified that he was "not ignorant of his [Satan's] devices," "lest Satan should get an advantage" of him (2 Corinthians 2:11). Satan seeks to gain a favorable and strategic place in the life of the believer to do him harm (Ephesians 6:11; 2 Thessalonians 2:9). Unless we acquaint ourselves with his wiles and subtle strategy, we are bound to fall under his attacks.

It is precisely the same idea that is conveyed by the injunction "Neither give place to the devil" (Ephesians 4:27). This warning against yielding ground or giving foothold to the devil was issued in reference to a number of sins (vv. 25-32), especially the sin of anger. Unless anger is truly righteous indignation and unless it is short-lived, it will degenerate into spite, revenge, and murder. This sin will open the way for a demon, as in the case of Cain, and drive one to awful hatred and even murder (vv. 26-27).

The opposite of giving place to the devil through any sin is resisting him, opposing his every advance. The promise is: "Resist the devil, and he will flee from you" (James 4.7). The satanic principle is to take as much ground as possible when not resisted.

Satan, who is called the believer's opponent, is compared to a lion on the prowl, roaring and ready at all times to pounce upon his prey and "devour" him (1 Peter 5:8). The figure is of the devil tearing his victim apart limb by limb and consuming him. Certainly this conveys the idea that the powers of darkness are able to make a very serious encroachment upon the life of a child of God. In fact, they go so far as to kill the body (Matthew 10:28). How dare a believer ignore this warning or naively tone down its terrifying implications?

Christians have received "the spirit which is of God" (1 Corinthians 2:12). But they are in danger of receiving "another" spirit of a "different" kind (a demon spirit), especially when encountering satanic delusion working in the religious realm (1 Timothy 4.1; 1 John 4:1-2; cf. 2 Thessalonians 2:2). This is exactly what Paul is saying in 2 Corinthians 11:4: "For if he that cometh preacheth another Jesus, whom ye have not preached, or if ye *receive another spirit*, which ye have not received, . . . ye might well bear with him."

Only by another spirit, that is, a spirit "different" from the Holy Spirit (a demon spirit), could one preach another (different) Jesus and "another [different] gospel" (Galatians 1:6-9). Such a proclaimer of "another Jesus" and "another gospel" can only be categorized as a false prophet. The apostle John solemnly warns the "beloved" of the peril of *believing* the "spirits" that are energizing false prophets (1 John 4:1).

The expression "receiving another" or "different spirit," therefore, means more than simply believing and receiving false teachers. It denotes believing and receiving the spirits "not of [from] God" (1 John 4:3), who energize *all* false teachers.

It is possible, then, for an unwary believer to be deluded religiously, to be trapped in false doctrine, and to become an earnest, diligent propagandist of the vagaries of some cult. In such a case he receives a spirit different in kind from the

Holy Spirit. The conclusion is inescapable; he receives an alien spirit.

The Holy Spirit is received to reside in the body. Likewise, a spirit "not of God" may be allowed to invade the body (1 John 4:3). This means that an evil spirit personality, though possibly religious, refined, and sophisticated, is granted entrance to work havoc alongside the Holy Spirit. This is hard for many Christians to understand. But why should it be difficult to understand in these last days of unparalleled religious confusion and delusion (1 Timothy 4:1)? It is the tragic picture of God's saints who are caught up in false doctrine and plundered by Satan working in the cults, parading as "an angel of light" and his human agents under demon dynamic "transformed as the ministers of righteousness" (2 Corinthians 11:14-15).

A Plea to Face Reality

In a demonic age when Satan and evil spiritual personalities are staging a colossal end-time demonstration of activity and power, Christians need to face the full implications of both Scripture and experience concerning exactly how far these evil agents can go in the case of regenerated humanity.

To deny the possibility of demonic working in the lives of Christians is to fail to allow Scripture to speak in the full scope of its implications and to flatly ignore experience. To fail to grasp the full extent to which such sinister power may operate is perilous, for it denies to those who have been invaded by the enemy the understanding and help they so desperately need. Also, this teaching warns those uninvaded of the peril of invasion and of what will happen if they fail to reckon on what they are in Christ and backslide into gross and willful sin.

A Bible Institute Student Delivered

The following case is that of a Christian woman, a student at the Missionary Training Institute at Nyack, New York, in the spring of 1951. The deliverance of this young woman is recounted by the Reverend J. A. MacMillan, a former missionary to the Orient and, at the time, an instructor at the institute, in a letter to Mrs. Lulu Gordon Cheesman. Like Mr. MacMillan, Mrs. Cheesman has for many years been widely used by God in dealing with the demon-oppressed.

Mrs. Cheesman sent me a copy of Mr. MacMillan's letter, which I quote:

JUNE 13, 1951

DEAR MRS. CHEESMAN:

There has been further development in the case mentioned in my last letter—you will be interested. Commencement was near at the school, and knowledge of the case had spread rapidly. It was decreed that the student must be delivered by a certain date or else must be removed from the buildings and the campus by that time. She came to my home crying bitterly, and as there seemed no other place, we took her in. Then the storm broke.

I have never seen anything like it nor have I heard of any similar experience. A number of students gave aid most willingly, and helped through the periods of convulsions which were at times most severe. On Wednesday, June 6th, the enemy attacked during united prayer about 5:00 P.M., the conflict lasting until the following afternoon without abatement. Demon after demon came out. The first group made various threats to kill her, and attacks of suffocation came which seemed as if the threat would be fulfilled. One demon seemed to be the master spirit, calling himself "Negro Trainer." He was the most powerful I have seen, and several strong men (G.I. students) had difficulty in controlling her.

During the attack just mentioned, this demon revealed himself, and after a hard struggle seemed to go. There followed a multitude of lesser spirits, who seemed connected with experiences she had undergone while employed in relief work in a mountain district. They narrated the most foul stories and talked with hilarity which made it most difficult to silence or control them. Eventually they were expelled. Then suddenly Negro Trainer appeared with a scornful "Ha! Ha! Ha! You thought I was gone, but here I am again." After a long struggle he seemed to go.

On Saturday noon without warning another attack came. She had barely time to cry out when the power seized her. A young man and a nurse were at hand, and I was at the scene in a few moments. Her struggles were intense, but quickly other helpers were at hand. Then began a struggle which lasted unbroken for eighteen hours, until 6:00 A.M. Sunday morning.

Again the attempt was made to suffocate her, the tongue sinking into the throat and respiration ceasing. A challenge as to the coming of Christ in the flesh would bring the tongue back, or commands to the demon to release it. Even the nurses feared for her life and often artificial respiration had to be used, but grace prevailed. Later on towards daylight a sudden attack of hysteria came in which she loudly wept, protesting that she was weary and unable to continue.

I saw it as a deception, though some of the helpers felt that I was wrong and that her physical state should be considered. But suddenly, as we continued to pray, the demon gave a great shout and released her. Immediately she became normal, protesting that she wished to be delivered at any cost.

During this time the demon had taunted us and sneered at us. He said, not like the others that he would kill her, but that he wanted her life and that if she would not be his servant he would take her when he left. When conscious she steadfastly stood with us, defying the demon and claiming victory through the blood of Christ. Through her wide-open eyes he looked at us with a look of the greatest terror. Gradually he weakened until his voice could hardly be heard. Again and again he appeared to leave with a gasp, until finally we could contact him no more. But he, or some other, is still within.

Since Sunday morning there has been no evidence of demon presence until yesterday. About noon I drove the nurse to the hospital, being away about ten minutes. During that time a sudden discouragement came upon her and she called for help, but when I came back this disappeared. The young man who was with her is most capable in handling the case. Just now he is reading to her the prayer tract you sent, and she is repeating it after him.

Each evening a group gathers for prayer that the deliverance may be complete. Today the power seemed to be building up within her, but it appears to be held in check. When the enemy is in control her face swells and the chest and abdomen seem also to enlarge. This is according to the old-time teaching of the *obh,* as mentioned by Pember and others. Perhaps we have learned more from this case than at any other time in the past. But we are heartily wearied of it, and pray for full deliverance. However, we feel that there is but one demon left—the total thus far reaching 171. He hides himself but must soon yield.

Letters keep coming, asking for help in similar matters from all over the land. Surely there is an incursion of spirits of evil pouring in upon us. How much Christians need to understand.

J. A. MacMillan

Later word from Mr. MacMillan reads:

This young woman was entirely set free with no further trouble whatever. She took hold of your prayer tract, Mrs. Chessman, with zeal and eagerness, and it was in reality the key to her deliverance. At first she repeated it after those who read it to her, and, as soon as she was able, she used it for herself to ward off attacks and found it fully effective. She went on with her work at the school with a fine mind and had no more trouble whatsoever.

Satan Is Alive but Defeated

The following account of a simple believer delivered from demon power comes from the north Amazon region of Brazil. It is told by missionary Steve Anderson and took place in the fall of 1968.

Yesterday I lay in a bushrope hammock in an Indian house, finishing a flash-card lesson on numbers. My loin-cloth-clad students were most enthusiastic.

Suddenly out leaped an old man from the other side of the donut-shaped building, dancing around the inner part. Barking dogs and their yelling masters began to harmonize with his sound of witching.

Carlos, the cause of all this commotion, lay in the oppo-site side of the house, struggling desparately in an acute at-tack of bronchitis. As I walked slowly but deliberately to him, I was aware of inquisitive faces peering out from the partitions.

Slipping through the crispy, dangling banana leaves that form the inner wall, I stepped up to Carlos as he sat stiff as a board, muttering unintelligible sounds.

My hands on his heaving shoulders, Carlos gasped, "Mi-han, Mihan." That my ears recognized very well—"Get away from there, get away from there." My eyes, smarting with smoke but otherwise good, saw nothing while it was obvious his glassy, staring eyes did.

I put my head down by the head of my brother in Christ who sat struggling for a bit of air. As I claimed the power of God, everything became quiet. So quiet, my prayer intended principally for the sick man, was heard by all within 25 feet. At first there was no response from Carlos. But as I commanded, in the name of Jesus, the Fekalap (demons) to leave immedi-ately, he groaned approval that seemed to sigh with relief.

Twenty hours later, Carlos looked at me in the dancing shadows of his fire . . . "When I was really sick, you sent the Fekalap away."

"Carlos, because God is powerful and because God loves you, I asked Him to chase away the demons that all of your people might see His Spirit work. That is why He made you well, Carlos."

Carlos testified that as we had talked to God, he saw the Fekalap fly away.

So went another enlightening experience in our spiritual warfare. It has given me a healthy respect for demons and a happy confidence in my all-powerful risen Lord.

8

DEMONIZATION IN ITS MILDER FORMS

It is my personal conviction that much of the confusion that exists today in the minds of many Christians concerning the question of how far demonic powers can go in the life of a truly regenerate person is due to failure to understand the strictly biblical terminology "to have a familiar spirit" (see Leviticus 20:27; Heb. "to be demonized" or "to have a demon," see below). As already noted in the previous chapter, the confusing term, so popularly employed to denote extreme demonization, is *demon possession.* But the Bible makes no distinction. *All* cases of demon invasion (having a demon or demons) are instances of demonization, no matter to what degree of mildness or severity. It appears, therefore, that the more precise biblical term is "demonization" (being demonized) rather than "demon possession" (possessed by a demon or demons).

THE OLD TESTAMENT CONCEPT

The law of Moses viewed fortune-tellers and spiritistic mediums as indwelt by one or more demons. These spirit personalities are called "familiar spirits" in the King James Version because they resided in the body of the witch medium and were on familiar ("family") terms with the human instrument in which they resided and through whom they worked.

Such spiritistic traffic involved insult and rebellion against the Lord. Hence the stem injunctions: "Turn ye not unto them that have familiar spirits nor unto the wizards; seek them not out, to be defiled by them: I am Jehovah your God" (Leviticus 19:31; ASV). The literal Hebrew is, "Turn ye not unto the familiar spirits," because the divining demons in the medium used the man or woman merely as an agent or go-between to bridge the gap between the natural world and the supernatural realm.

"And the soul that turneth unto them that have familiar spirits [lit., "unto the familiar spirits"], and unto the wizards, to play the harlot after them, I will even set my face against that soul, and will cut him off from among his people" (Leviticus 20:6; ASV).

The most revealing verse is Leviticus 20:27—"A man also or a woman that hath a familiar spirit [lit., "in whom there is a divining demon"], or that is a wizard, shall surely be put to death: they shall stone them with stones: their blood shall be upon them."

The "wizard" is properly the "knowing one," as both the Hebrew and English words denote. The demon indwelling the medium is the source of the supernatural knowledge. The Greek-derived word "demon" is defined by Plato from an adjective formed from the root *dao*, signifying "knowing" or "intelligent," and points to the superior knowledge of these spirit beings.[1] Hence, demons are able, as a result of their indwelling, to grant oracular and clairvoyant powers.

The medium of Endor, whom King Saul consulted oracularly, is described as "a woman that hath a familiar spirit [lit., a woman controlled by a fortune-telling demon]" 1 Samuel 28:7). It is obvious that all such occult workers are indwelt by demonic powers and can be said to be demonized, that is, subjected to various degrees of control by a demon or demons.

The New Testament Concept

The common idea of demon indwelling in the New Testament is expressed by a Greek word, *daimonizomai*, signifying "to be demonized." The word means "to be under the power of a demon."[2]

This expression admits of great latitude, as noted briefly in the preceding sections, and clearly comprehends the various degrees of demon invasion. Since demons vary greatly in power and wickedness, their influence would of necessity differ in severity and manner of manifestation (Matthew 4:24; 8:16, 28, 33; 9:32; 12:22; 15:22; Mark 1:32; 5:15; Luke 8:36; John 10:21).

Another expression "to have a demon," is used in the New Testament. In certain cases the evil spirit was the cause of some physical or mental aberration (Luke 4:33; 8:27). This does not mean that the New Testament attributes all mental or physical maladies to demon power. Actually it distinguishes those caused by a demon from natural disorders (cf. Matthew 4:24; 8:16; Mark 1:32; Luke 8:2; Acts 5:16; 8:7).

The phrase "to have a demon" is also employed of those who act and speak irrationally, as if they were mad (Matthew 11:18; Luke 7:33; John 7:20; 8:48; 10:20). But such usage, signifying invasion, does imply actual demonization.

The Situation Today

Despite the present-day revival of occultism, particularly since the dawn of the so-called age of Aquarius in 1970,[3] there still exists a widespread error that demons and demonization just do not exist. Scientific progress and human enlightenment, it is contended, have united to banish such superstitions from men's minds.[4] But those who are spiritually perceptive realize that such a position is simply falling to the devil's cleverest wile to deceive people into thinking that he does not exist.

Satan and demons not only existed in Bible times, they exist today. In fact, the powers of darkness are enjoying a heyday in the occult movements and Satan worship that are springing up like mushrooms in these last days. The immense popularity of books, movies, and TV shows dealing with occult themes—such as *The Exorcist*, the *Friday the 13th* movies and TV serial, and Stephen King's novels and movies—attest to the presence and power of the demonic in today's society.

The spread of witchcraft, astrology, tarot cards, fortune-telling, Ouija boards, séances, witches, clairvoyants, and devil worship is a worldwide phenomenon. The enormous increase of the cults, the invasion of Christianity by demonized religion, the importation of Oriental mystical religions, and the uncritical acceptance of the New Age movement all attest to the powerful working of demonic forces in today's world. Added to this peril is the colossal threat of atheistic, materialistic Communism that enslaves over one billion of the earth's population.

These conditions presage a fearful demonization of society. Few would controvert the danger unsaved humanity faces, yet many are hazy concerning precisely what, if anything, satanic forces can do to the regenerate, especially where serious sin and backsliding are involved or where occult participation becomes a factor. In such cases can a demon enter and indwell a believer? Can such a believer, if he persists in sin or reverts to his preconversion way of life, ever become more dangerously demonized?

Demonic Invasion and the Believer

Those who deny the possibility of a demon invading a believer run the risk of believing the devil's lie that he will not enter if permitted, or they assume that the believer loses his moral choice in the matter and cannot open the door to demonic powers. It is most emphatically true that the believer cannot open the door to the powers of darkness with respect to his salvation, which assures his *position* in Christ before God. This is *entirely* God's work, and *no* creature, including Satan and the demons, can touch it (1 John 5:18; NASB).

But the believer most surely can open the door to demonic powers with respect to his *experience* of his position before God in Christ. His experience is conditioned upon recognition of his position and upon his faith to make it real in his everyday living (Romans 6:11).

If the believer is ignorant of his position and fails to reckon on it, Satan and demons are ready to take full advantage. Serious sin in the believer gives them the opportunity to exert their power in the Christian's experience. This means they will work outside the body if they can do no better. They prefer, however, to work from within. That is why they bid high to try to enter and gain entrance into the believer's life as a squatter.

MILD DEMONIC INVASION

Many Christians overlook the fact that demonic agents vary greatly in power. Some are "principalities," or five-star generals, commanders-in-chief in Satan's vast army of spirit rebels; others are "powers" of lesser rank, but still colonels and captains over the devil's hosts; then there are "rulers of the darkness of this world," literally "age rulers of this darkness," who exert wide influence in the government of the satanic world system; others are only buck-private demons, "the spiritual forces of wickedness," who operate widely and in such a varied manner in the realm of evil supernaturalism (Ephesians 6:12; NASB). Obviously, in cases of mild invasion, demons of lesser rank and power are involved.

But it is often forgotten that demons not only differ greatly in power and influence but also in degree of depravity as well. Jesus spoke of a demon spirit who left his abode but then returned, bringing with him "seven other spirits more wicked than himself" (Matthew 12:45).

There is a widespread tendency today to view all demons as dirty, nasty, and viciously immoral. Of course many are. Such depraved demons can enslave only those people who allow their minds to be debased by pornography and who give themselves up to lewdness and sexual license of every sort.

But many demons are nice, refined, religious, and "good" in a self-righteous sense. They are perfectly at home in a religion that rejects the gospel of salvation by faith and substitutes the devil's false gospel of salvation by works and extols human goodness as procuring acceptance before God (cf. 1 Timothy 4:1-2).

The fact is, there is only *one criterion* that differentiates "spirits not from God" (demons) from "spirits from God" (angels). The former oppose the Word and will of God, while the latter espouse and publish it abroad (1 John 4:1-2). Never does the Bible suggest the indwelling of the good angels. They have a varied ministry to the saints but do not control and indwell as does the Holy Spirit. If the elect angels did control believers, that would constitute usurpation of God's child by another creature. Indeed, this is what actually happens in the case of demon spirits, and it constitutes no inconsiderable part of their wicked lawlessness as fallen, depraved spirits.

Apart from their opposition to God and His Word, many demonic spirits are scarcely distinguishable from the Holy Spirit and the elect unfallen angels. This is precisely why the Spirit of God gives a sensitive acid test that centers in the person of our Lord and radiates out to every doctrine of our holy faith, like the concentric waves created by a stone thrown into the water (1 John 4:2).

Is it to be assumed that these "good," "religious" demons are limited only to influence and obsession *from without?* What about believers who become ensnared in heresy and depart from the faith? They actually take up with "seducing [wandering] spirits," who have strayed from the Word and will of God and espouse "doctrines of devils [demons]." Is it logical to assume that such heretical believers who speak "lies in hypocrisy" and have "their conscience seared with a hot iron" (1 Timothy 4:1-2) are arbitrarily protected from demon control?

Scripture emphatically sets no such artificial limits. Certainly experience does not. Any believer who has had to deal with truly born-again people who have become ensnared in some doctrine of demons and who have landed in some phase of perverted Christianity, *know* the power of the demon. Especially deceptive is the religious, even "super spiritual," variety, which speaks and operates *from within* its victim.

Besides the power and the degree of depravity of demons, their number and extent of influence on a person's life are also factors to be considered in defining the nature of their control and its distinction from more severe cases of demonization.

Both Scripture and experience attest that the demonized condition may be caused by one or many demons (cf. Matthew 12:43-45; Mark 5:8-13). This is obviously an important factor in assessing all instances of demonization, whether in the case of sinner or saint.

It is well known that the degree to which a demon may exercise control over a person varies greatly. Jesus Himself declared that some evil spirits come out only as a result of fasting and protracted prayer (Matthew 17:21; Mark 9:29). Others are cast out with comparative ease. These facts are abundantly attested by those who counsel and deal with the demonically afflicted (Acts 5:16; 8:7; 19:12).[5]

CASES OF MILD DEMONIZATION

Mild demonic affliction is perhaps more widespread than is often supposed. I recall a case in one of my earlier pastorates that appears to fit in this category. The subject was a born-again woman, the mother of four children, all of whom were members of my church.

Never for a moment did I suspect demon inhabitation. This woman was exemplary in prayer and faithfulness. However, there was some indefinable power controlling her at times that made her, despite her love for the Lord, a continued source of confusion and agitation, particularly with other women in the church. So severe was this disturbing spirit that more than once it threatened the future of the church.

This situation continued unabated for several years. Then one evening during an unusually blessed prayer meeting we were praying around in a circle. When it was this woman's turn to pray, she prayed quietly and movingly, as was her custom. All of a sudden she gave vent to an incredible piercing, loud cry that almost scared us out of our wits. Immediately she gently rolled over and lost consciousness for about a minute. When she regained consciousness, she said, "I feel as if something evil has left me."

Indeed, a demon, which had invaded this woman and had by its evil presence created continual confusion in the work of God, had left, never to return. This servant of the Lord continued in her life of faith and prayer. But the disturbing spirit that had harassed us through her was no longer present to trouble her or us. She was set free when the power of prayer became too much for the demonic presence to bear.

Often we read in Scripture of this very thing. At Samaria, under Philip's ministry, "unclean spirits, crying with loud voice, came out of many that were possessed with them" (Acts 8:7; cf. Luke 4:41).

Cases of mild demonization are most common, it would appear, among true believers ensnared in false doctrine. The apostle John warns the "beloved" people of God, who are often very gullible, against the peril of listening to and believing "every spirit." For this reason he urges them to test the spirits to see whether they are from God or are demon spirits not from God.

The latter energize "false prophets" (1 John 4:1). While perhaps most false prophets never were saved, there is no warrant for assuming that none of them were. Certainly it is possible for the "beloved" people of God to receive a false spirit and to be led away into error.

In fact, in warning the Corinthians against false teachers, the apostle Paul suggests this very danger.

> But I fear, lest by any means, as the serpent beguiled Eve through his subtilty [craftiness], so your mind should be corrupted from the simplicity that is in Christ. For if he that cometh preacheth another Jesus, whom we have not preached, or if ye *receive another* spirit [a demon spirit], which ye have not received, or another gospel, which ye have not accepted ye might well bear with him. (2 Corinthians 11:3-4)

If it is objected that this Scripture does not refer to demon invasion but to listening to false teachers, it may be replied that listening to false teachers is really listening to the demon spirits who are influencing them (cf. 1 John 4:1). Listening leads to believing, which in turn results in receiving (opening the life to entry and eventual demonization).

The legalizing teachers, who dogged Paul's footsteps and opposed so violently his stand on the true gospel of grace through faith, were indisputably saved and "brothers" in the Lord. Yet, they had manifestly received "another [different] spirit" (2 Corinthians 11:4) than the Holy Spirit. This was the dynamic of their destructive ministry that caused the apostle Paul so much anguish (cf. Philippians 3:2-3). In combating erroneous teaching that denied the taking out of the church before the Tribulation, Paul refers to the danger of being shaken in mind and thrown into confusion "by [a] spirit," by which is meant "a deceiving demon spirit" since the threat of unsound doctrine is the issue (2 Thessalonians 2:2).

Paul warns the Corinthian believers against complicity with demon-energized paganism and idolatry (1 Corinthians

10:20). Compromise here may spell "fellowship with demons." This can only mean broken fellowship with the Holy Spirit and communion with an evil spirit. To limit this peril to demon influence from without seems arbitrary.

If believers revert to idolatry and its twin sister occultism, "fellowship with demons" and eventually demon invasion become inevitable. Today, Christians who dabble even innocently in witchcraft, spiritism, astrology, and fortune-telling cannot escape the inflexible laws of the spiritual realm. These laws are just as binding as those in the natural realm.

You play with demon-ridden occultism. You cease resisting the devil (James 4:8). You actually open the door to him and invite in his emissaries. Dare you assume they cannot enter? You will soon find out that they know they can enter and will promptly do so.

If you flirt with pornography, some satanic powers will corrupt and enslave your mind. It is an easy step from there to bind your life with lustful cravings that will enslave your body in sin with far deeper tyranny than the old nature could effect apart from demon power.

Recently a veteran missionary from Japan related the example of a fellow worker on the field who came under the enslavement of an unclean spirit. The spirit gained entrance when the missionary yielded to temptation and began visiting a pornographic bookstore in Tokyo.

Yielding to the temptation and cultivating the sin of lust, the missionary became enslaved by a demon of uncleanness. Fortunately, he repented in time, and through prayer he was delivered. Otherwise, total shipwreck of his life and ministry would have been inescapable.

It was my privilege to participate with several other believers in a prayer session on behalf of a young born-again man who was severely troubled by demonic powers harassing him. Only as the demons were faced, forced to give their names, and challenged through the power of God's Word and on the basis of Christ's shed blood did it turn out that vile spirits of lust were the most vexing and, in this case, the most resistant.

Only as the victim was commanded to come out of the demonized state of unconsciousness into which he had lapsed at the beginning of the prayer battle, and then as he consciously and firmly renounced any ground he had given the devil to invade his life and reassert his position in Christ, did these "unclean spirits" (cf. Mark 5:8-9) depart from him with frightful cries and horrible chokings.

In the spring of 1974 I was a speaker at a prophetic conference at the Church of the Open Door in Los Angeles, California. After I had given a message on demonic manifestations in the saved and the unsaved and had returned home to the East Coast, I received a letter from a Christian woman who had heard my message and was troubled with demon voices and other demonic phenomena.

In her earlier life she had dabbled in the occult, trying automatic writing, astrology, fortune-telling by cards, the Ouija board, and other things. She thought that there was little or nothing to all of this because of an almost complete lack of results.

Later on in life, however, she awoke to the danger of the occult when she began having clairvoyant dreams and hearing strange inner voices. In May 1970, when she began to seek help from the Lord but before she became a born-again believer, the demons began to harass her day and night, fearfully and piteously. She wrote:

> I hear several demon voices. One says his name is Ishmael. I think they just make up their names. At the time it started I didn't even believe demons existed.
>
> One morning as I awoke I heard an angry voice saying, "Christ is dead." At first I thought the voices I heard were neighbors or members of the family. Then I thought it must be mental telepathy (something I had tried with some success). The last thing I would have believed was that I had heard a demon.

Before I accepted Christ as my Lord and Savior in May, 1972, I lost the faith I thought I had. I thought I was supposed to follow the Law. As a lost sinner, I, of course, could not do that. The Law simply convicts of sin and shows us how much we need the Savior.

Graphically this woman recounted how the demons had fought her desperately to keep her away from saving faith in Christ and, after she was saved, to lure her away from trusting in Christ and what she had become in union with Him.

I am now saved by grace. Thanks be to God. I believe His Word. I have been studying the Word of God with the help of good radio teachers on KGER (Dr. Vernon McGee for one).

I thought it in the will of God to command the demons to depart from me and not to bother me anymore. I pray to God in Christ's name for help.

These demons have threatened me, my family, and even the dogs. Please pray for me. I would not have believed anyone who told me that they heard demons! I would have thought that they suffered from auditory hallucinations.

I heard a demon say, "She heard Jehovah damn her." Another said, "She will commit suicide."

I reject their lying voices. But they vex me, and I am a born-again child of God! I do not know what to do. Please HELP ME!

This pitiful cry of distress from a truly regenerated child of God is being multiplied over and over again in these last days, before the Lord's coming, when demonic powers are working to prepare the world for the rise of the Antichrist and the Great Tribulation.

How shall we answer such a cry of distress? Certainly not under the naive assumption that no true child of God can be demonized. Only by facing the problem with an open mind concerning what the Word of God has to say on the subject, and then conducting a spiritual warfare (Ephesians

6:10-20) based on what we are in Christ, can we face reality in this realm.

Christ's salvation is the basis of complete deliverance from demon power. Let us show people the way of full deliverance!

9

MODERATE AND SEVERE DEMONIZATION

Realistically facing the question of how far Satan and demons can go in the life of a seriously sinning saint is bound to arouse opposition from some believers. But the question presses for an answer: Has God set a limit in the experience of a believer beyond which demonic powers cannot go, even if the Christian deliberately *goes on sinning* scandalously and immorally?

MODERATE DEMONIZATION

Obviously more moderate demonization, like the milder varieties, depends on the power, number, degree of wickedness, and degree of influence of the demon spirits in the life. However, numerous factors on the human side also must be considered. Heredity, environment, upbringing, the degree to which the moral Law of God has been violated, complicity with sins of the flesh and spirit, and occult participation are only a few of them.

In considering the believer in relation to demonic phenomena, it must be remembered that when God saves us, He does not strip us of our will or constitute us robots or automatons. He leaves us with our wills renewed and set free to make right choices, but we are still free moral agents. We can choose the wrong.

Since we still have the old sin nature alongside the new nature, we can sin against God's holiness and rebel against His will. Although God chastens and scourges us (1 Corinthians 11:30-32; Hebrews 12:1-8), we can still persist in sin and rebellion to such a degree that God cuts off our physical life (1 Corinthians 5:1-5; 1 John 5:16-19).

In fact, that God uses Satan and demonic powers as a whip to chasten His disobedient sons is emphasized in Scripture. The ultimate is allowing Satan to take away our physical life (1 Corinthians 5:5; 1 John 5:16). The stages in between comprise the various degrees of demonization. The powers of darkness can work havoc in our changeable experience before men (1 Corinthians 11:30-32). But as we have constantly pointed out, they can never touch our unalterable position before God (1 John 5:18; NASB).

Christians, then, cannot only sin; they can sin scandalously and recklessly. When they do sin and then fail to respond to God's chastening in confession, they progressively expose themselves to the powers of darkness, first from without, and then, if they willfully persist, from within. It is this latter predicament that eventually causes spiritual shipwreck and the premature end of their career on earth.

Hymenaeus and Alexander were two "shipwrecked" believers that apparently fit this category. They failed to hold to "faith, and a good conscience." Paul "delivered [them] unto Satan" that they might "learn not to blaspheme" (1 Timothy 1:19-20). Evidently they had persisted far into sin and rebellion to speak evil or curse God (Romans 2:24; Titus 2:5). Perhaps they had railed against and maliciously denied the work of the Holy Spirit (Matthew 12:31).

There is every intimation that these two believers came under severe demonic control and bondage. Opening their lives to Satan, the powers of darkness entered.

Paul apparently refers to the same believer later when he declares, "Alexander the coppersmith did me much harm; the Lord will repay him according to his deeds" (2 Timothy

4:14; NASB). Paul warns of the dangerous state to which this believer had sunk when he says, "Be on guard against him yourself, for he vigorously opposed our teaching" (v. 15; NASB).

Alexander's fanatical opposition to God's Word preached by Paul displays the severe demonic power he was under. Rebellion against God's Word and will, it must be emphasized, marks the one criterion that distinguishes a good spirit from a demon spirit.

The apostle Paul also refers to Hymenaeus together with Philetus as being guilty of destructive heresy and speech that spreads like gangrene: "But avoid worldly and empty chatter, for it will lead to further ungodliness, and their talk will spread like gangrene. Among them are Hymenaeus and Philetus, men who have gone astray from the truth saying that the resurrection has already taken place, and thus they upset the faith of some" (2 Timothy 2:16-18; NASB).

Evidently the legalistic Jewish believers of the church of Smyrna (Revelation 2:8-11) and Philadelphia (Revelation 3:7-13), like the legalizing brethren that hounded Paul's steps, also belonged to this category. Their condition was patently more severe than mere demon influence or even a mild invasion. They are castigated as liars and blasphemers. Their evil is directly connected with the powers of darkness, fearfully propagating doctrines that slandered God's grace and the complete efficacy of Christ's finished redemptive work, and erroneous teachings like the legalism the apostle Paul uses as an example of "doctrines of demons" (1 Timothy 4:1-6; NASB).

The question arises in these instances of flagrant heresy as to whether a believer can lapse into "doctrines of demons" and propagate them with abandon and fanatical zeal and not come under demon control. It seems safer to interpret such unholy zeal and rabid animosity against the truth of God as energized by spirits who have invaded these false teachers.

As a result, these turncoat brethren are consigned to "the synagogue," not of Jewish believers, as they claimed to be, but "of Satan" (Revelation 2:9; 3:9). Their whole activity as believers has an indelible demonic impress. Their conduct seems explainable only on the basis of entrenchment of evil spirits deep in their personality.

Similarly, the believers in the church at Thyatira who tolerated paganistic teachings taught by the self-styled prophetess, Jezebel, obviously came under dangerous demonic control. "She teaches and leads *My bond-servants* astray, so that they commit acts of immorality and eat things sacrificed to idols" (Revelation 2:20; NASB). As the Lord's "bond-servants," they are certainly to be taken as genuine believers.

The fact that, though God gave these believers "time to repent," they did "not want to repent" of their "immorality" demonstrates what a strong hold the demon powers had over them and the scourging, even to death, that they had to endure (Revelation 2:21-23; NASB). Such language would be pointless apart from genuine believers who had defected.

Those in Thyatira who held these doctrines of demons plumbed "the deep things of Satan" (Revelation 2:24; NASB). This can only mean that they came under enslaving demonic sway and were invaded by the powers of darkness. Certainly indicated is implication in occultism, which is inseparable from the paganism Jezebel taught (cf. 1 Corinthians 10:20). The inevitable result was "fellowship with demons," as communion with the Holy Spirit was forfeited. It seems that plumbing "the deep things of Satan," which results in fellowshiping with demons, refers to severe demonization.

To conclude that these instances are representative of unsaved people is gratuitous when they are addressed as the Lord's "bond-servants" (Revelation 2:20; NASB) under the category of churches among which Christ walks (v. 1). Besides, such an assumption avoids the difficulties and solves no problems. It allows theory to be untested fully by facts. The result is theoretical doctrine that does not realistically reflect the full scope of revealed truth on the matter, nor jibe with authenticated human experience.

OTHER APPARENT CASES OF SATANIC INWORKING

The sin of Ananias and Sapphira (Acts 5:1-11) furnished an inlet for the powers of darkness. But it is not easy from the data presented to define theologically precisely what took place. The sin of these believers was not holding back part of their property. It consisted of lying to the Holy Spirit about the matter (Acts 5:4-5).

Prompted by the Holy Spirit to give the full price of the possession they sold, they told God that is what they would do. But in holding back part of the price and then pretending they gave the full amount, they lied to God (Acts 5:4). Satan, the "liar, and the father of lies" (John 8:44; NASB), "filled" their hearts "to lie to the Holy Spirit" (Acts 5:3; NASB). The same word used of the believer who is "filled with the Spirit" (*plēroō*) is employed here of Ananias, whom the powers of darkness "filled" (Ephesians 5:18).

Ananias's and Sapphira's deaths constituted "an evident act of judgment—the judgment that begins at the house of God."[1] This is obviously the "sin unto [physical] death," the ultimate in God's chastening of a sinning saint (1 John 5:16). It entails being "delivered" or handed over to Satan's power for "the destruction of . . . [the] flesh [physical death]," that the "spirit may be saved in the day of the Lord Jesus" (1 Corinthians 5:5; NASB).

God often uses Satan and the demonic powers as a sharp whip to scourge His seriously sinning saints. The Father's purpose in thus disciplining a disobedient son is for the son's temporal and eternal good. His aim is to rescue the son from shipwreck and disaster in this life and, failing this, to preserve him for heaven in the life to come.

Also at stake in the sin of Ananias and Sapphira was the honor and integrity of the whole Christian community. The punishment of these two furnished a stern warning to the entire church as to how the sin of one member affects the whole Body of Christ (Acts 5:11; 1 Corinthians 12:25-26).

Similar in its gravity and effect upon the Lord's people was the sin of Achan (Joshua 7:11-12). He "sinned against the Lord God of Israel" (Joshua 7:20). In doing so, he caused Israel to sin and to suffer shameful defeat before her enemies (Joshua 7:1-10). Just as Satan the liar filled Ananias's and Sapphira's hearts to lie to God, so he, the archrebel against God (Isaiah 14:12-14), filled Achan's heart to rebel against God. What was solemnly commanded by God to be utterly destroyed or completely devoted to the Lord, Achan, with brazen-faced disobedience and deception, kept for himself (Joshua 7:21).

It is true that the account does not delineate the unseen spiritual struggle behind the scenes. Nevertheless, it was just as real an invasion of the heart by the powers of darkness of this seriously sinning Old Testament saint as in the case of Ananias and Sapphira in the New Testament. Presumably Achan's awful sin exposed him directly to Satan's power. More than this cannot be said because God's Word says no more.

The terrible feud between Abimelech and the Shechemites is another example of the entrance of an evil spirit among the Lord's people to cause tragic division. God sent this "evil spirit" to punish Abimelech for his cruelty in murdering Gideon's seventy sons and the men of Shechem for helping him in this awful crime (Judges 9:23-24).

OTHER POSSIBLY MORE SEVERE CASES OF DEMONIC INWORKING

Recent linguistic research suggests that the case of Cain, the first murderer, is to be classified in this category. The grammatical difficulties of the Hebrew text of Genesis 4:7 are removed by viewing the word rendered "crouching"

(*robes*), not as a participle modifying "sin," but as an Akkadi-
an loan word meaning "demon" (*rabisum*): "If you do well,
will not your countenance be lifted up? And if you do not
well, sin is *a demon* at the door; and its [the demon's] desire
is for you, but you must master it [the demon]."

Not only does this rendering remove the ambiguities of
the Hebrew text, as heretofore interpreted, but clarifies the
satanic dynamic behind Cain's awful act and subsequent career in going out "from the presence of the Lord" (Genesis
4:8, 16), suggesting that in his early life he might have been a
genuine believer.

The sin of Aaron's sons, Nadab and Abihu, was very serious because it occasioned physical death (Leviticus 10:1-
5). These men were believers because they were redeemed
out of Egypt and were priests in Israel. Like Achan's sin and
the sin of Ananias and Sapphira, theirs was definitely an affront to God, in either flagrantly rebelling against Him or im-
pudently lying to Him. There is no other conclusion than that
the same powers of darkness filled the heart of one as did the
other. This is true despite the fact that the Old Testament narratives assume but do not describe the spiritual conflict behind the scenes.

The "strange," unauthorized fire offered by Nadab and
Abihu represented the sin of acting in the things of God apart
from His revealed will. It was a variation of the same sin of
rebellion that Achan committed. It was very serious, but
whether it involved demon indwelling can only be presumed
from its seriousness. Further than this the biblical evidence
does not go.

Fire "from before the Lord" (Leviticus 9:24) had initially
kindled the flame upon the altar of burnt offering. The priests
were responsible to keep this burning (Leviticus 6:12-13). No
specific directions had yet been given as to how the incense
should be lit.

Aaron's sons acted presumptuously, in self-will, and ig-
nited the incense in their own way without consulting God. It

was an instance of "will worship" (Colossians 2:23), rebellion against God's Word and will in religious things.

Korah's sin was also a variation of open rebellion against the divine order (Numbers 16:1-50; Jude 1:11). It was a bold, God-defying intrusion into the priests' office. The Lord had clearly stipulated that only Aaron and his sons were to assume this office (cf. Hebrews 5:4). The terrible fate of these rebels, as the earth opened up and swallowed them, demonstrates the seriousness of their sin and its deep demonic nature. It was evidently a delivering over to satanic powers for the destruction of physical life (cf. 1 Corinthians 5:5; 1 John 5:16). That the sin involved demon invasion can only be presumed from its heinousness, for such is not actually stated.

The career of Balaam (Numbers 22-24) offers a strange mixture of occultism with the worship and service of God. As a pagan diviner of repute, Balaam of necessity was energized as a clairvoyant and soothsayer by demon powers, as are all occultists who operate in the realm of evil supernaturalism. Yet, despite the fact that he was contaminated by occult religion and an enemy of Israel, God raised him up, at least temporarily, to the status of a true prophet of the Lord:"The spirit of God came upon him" (Numbers 24.2).[2]

Balaam illustrates the fact that the Spirit of God may work in believers who are weak in faith and deficient in sound doctrine. However, it must be remembered that the Spirit of God *never* indicates nor empowers false doctrine. Doctrinal errors are "doctrines of demons" (1 Timothy 4:1; NASB; cf. 1 John 4.1-2). All unsound teaching is originated and propagated by demon spirits, emphatically *not* by the Holy Spirit.

This can only mean that when false doctrine is subscribed to and followed, the work of the Holy Spirit is hindered, perverted, and vitiated in proportion to the extent to which demonic powers are permitted to influence from without or allowed entrance to work from within. The situation that results depends upon how serious are the errors espoused and to what degree they control the believer.

Balaam offers a dramatic example of how the Holy Spirit may work in and speak through one who evidently knows the Almighty, yet is woefully contaminated by occult religion. Accordingly, it seems hard to conclude otherwise than that the Spirit of God spoke through Balaam, at least on occasion, despite the fact that he, at the same time, was energized by demon powers. In his case these dark powers seemed to have complete control over him since he was so thoroughly contaminated by divination and other forms of idolatrous paganism (cf. Numbers 23:15; 24:1).

The case of Balaam sheds light on a vexing question of our day. Many truly born-again believers are being entrapped in the false teachings and cults of Christianity. As a result they are coming under strong demon influence and obsession from without and, in more pronounced cases, actually suffering from demons working from within. The problem is, how can the Spirit of God indwell and work in these believers at the same time they are influenced by demonic spirits?

That the Spirit of God worked in Balaam seems undeniable. His parables form a high-water mark in Old Testament poetry and Messianic prophecy. The beauty and spiritual depth of these utterances of Balaam undeniably came from the Spirit of God breathing through him. That the Holy Spirit can work in born-again believers who are caught in some forms of error seems equally certain. The answer to the anomaly is that the Holy Spirit operates, insofar as He can, empowering whatever truth the believer may possess. However, his work is hindered and seriously warped by doctrinal errors that give demons the power to distort the thinking and conduct of those ensnared in erroneous teachings.

The modern-day, widely spreading charismatic movement in the church offers a striking example. In general, it represents a true movement of the Holy Spirit in revival and spiritual renewal. But the doctrinal errors and inaccuracies upon which it is erected offer an inlet to demon spirits. Instigating and propagating the unsound teachings ("doctrines of demons") it fosters, spirits not of God (1 John 4:1-2) spoil the underlying work of the Spirit of God.

Evidences of demonic spoiling of the Holy Spirit's work in salvation and revival are evident. These include divisions and misunderstandings among God's people, obscuration of the gospel of grace, miscomprehension of what salvation is, forefeiture of security and stability in Christian living, and robbing the believer of his maturity in Christ, thus reducing him to a state of infancy and immaturity.

EXPLICIT CASES OF SEVERE INVASION

The case of King Saul, already mentioned,[3] is of such importance to require more detailed consideration under the category of more obviously severe demonization. That Saul was a regenerated Old Testament believer can scarcely be denied. The Spirit of the Lord came upon him and he was "turned into another man" (1 Samuel 10:6). He prophesied on one occasion with the Lord's prophets, and at the beginning of his career God was declared to be with him (1 Samuel 10:7-11). He performed exploits under God's blessing as the Spirit of God came upon him (1 Samuel 10:6, 10). He also built an altar to the Lord (1 Samuel 14:35).

But he early exhibited a stubborn spirit of rebellion against the Lord. He intruded into the priest's office, like the rebel Korahites (1 Samuel 13:8-13), and he also refused to execute fully God's commands concerning the Amalekites (1 Samuel 15:1-35). The result was that he not only forefeited God's blessing, but he invited stern divine disciplinary action. He lost permanent hold on the kingship and so grieved and quenched the Spirit that he became harassed by a demon spirit that periodically took control of him (1 Samuel 16:14).

That this was a divine chastisement is indicated by the fact that the intruder is called "an evil spirit from the Lord." The meaning is that a demon was used by the Lord to whip the erring king for his flagrant disobedience. The passage is an illustration of the truth we have been emphasizing, that God uses the powers of darkness as His instruments to discipline His wayward children.

Saul's case represents extremely serious rebellion against the Lord in the realm of *both* the priesthood and the kingship. It is on a par with Nadab and Abihu's transgression and the revolt of the sons of Korah in the sphere of the priesthood. The divine order set in these offices was absolutely fixed and unalterably set. Such offices represented the Lord in these spheres as the One who changes not (Malachi 3:6).

For man to introduce change according to human will (Nadab and Abihu) or to set aside God's unalterable order (the Korahites) or to brush aside the command of the heavenly King for the self-will of His earthly representative (King Saul) constitutes the quintessence of the satanic spirit of opposition to the Word and will of God.

King Saul, like others similarly afflicted, was not always under the control of the demon that was demonizing him. Only upon occasion did he lapse into the demonized state. Then, when the evil spirit was "on" him (i.e., when he lapsed into the demonized state), he was ill-tempered and violent. The demon "terrorized him" (1 Samuel 16:14-15; NASB).

On such occasions David would play his harp. Doubtless the young musician performed some of the beautiful psalms of praise to the Lord, which were unpalatable to the evil spirit. Hence, it would leave and thus be unable to terrorize its victim. "And Saul would be refreshed and be well" (1 Samuel 16:23; NASB).

When David returned from killing Goliath and the women sang greater praise to David than to the king, Saul's jealousy permitted full demonic access to his life. "An evil spirit from God came mightily upon Saul, and he raved in the midst of the house" (1 Samuel 18:10; NASB).

It was while David was playing the harp before the king that Saul demonstrated the severe demonic control he was under. Taking the spear he held in his hand, he hurled it in violent anger and uncontrollable jealousy at David, seeking to pin him to the wall (1 Samuel 18:l0-ll; cf. 19:10).

These spells were frequent, for David escaped such a violent attack on his life twice. The cruel way in which the king tried to hunt down David like a wild animal to slay him illustrates the terrible demon power the rebellious king had come under. Saul's final act of outrageous revolt against the Lord, that of having recourse to a spiritistic medium when God no longer would communicate with him, was the prelude to his sin unto physical death on the battlefield of Gilboa (1 Samuel 28:4-25; 31:

Saul's career is a dramatic reminder of how the powers of darkness can destroy the testimony and life of a blatantly disobedient saint. Anointed of the Lord, given a new heart, and initially showing great promise, Saul made shipwreck of his life. Although he was an Old Testament believer and did not enjoy the New Testament position and the protection of the permanent indwelling of the Spirit, he stands as a solemn warning. The Spirit, seriously grieved by sin (Ephesians 4:30) and quenched by gross disobedience (1 Thessalonians 5:19), can offer no barrier to the invasion of satanic forces. They know how far they can go, and they go every inch they are allowed.

Even King David, because of his terrible sin of murder and adultery, barely escaped such shipwreck. He avoided demonic despoilment because he promptly confessed his sin before the Lord and did not persist in his iniquity. Consequently Nathan could say to him, "The Lord also has taken away your sin; you shall not die. However, because by this deed you have given occasion to the enemies of the Lord to blaspheme, the child also that is born to you shall surely die" (2 Samuel 12:13-14; NASB). And not only did the child born of sin die. The crimes David had committed honeycombed his family, causing him to pay in bitter suffering and remorse the rest of his days on earth.

One of the clearest and most extended passages on demon activity among religious people catalogs the case of the four hundred prophets of Ahab (1 Kings 22:1-40). As already noted,[4] Micaiah, the son of Imlah, was hardly the only true prophet of the Lord. They all consulted Jehovah, the God of Israel, not the Canaanite deity, Baal.

"These four hundred are not to be identified with Jezebel's four hundred prophets of Baal, whom Elijah had slain (1 Kings 18:40). These men were ostensibly prophets of the Lord, as Jehoshaphat's willingness to seek their counsel shows," declares J. T. Gates.[5] Professor William Sanford LaSor says they were "obviously prophets of Yahweh and not of Baal, yet they were subsidized by the king and therefore said what he wanted to hear."[6]

Presumptive evidence is not that none of these prophets of the Lord were believers, but that some of them (if not the majority of them) were believers. But despite the fact that they were the Lord's prophets, they became controlled by deceptive spirits because of base compromise to please the renegade Ahab (1 Kings 22:19-22).

The narrative plainly declares that these prophets thought they were telling the truth by the Spirit of God. When the demon-controlled Zedekiah came near and struck the Spirit-controlled Micaiah on the cheek, he was not joking when he said, "How did the Spirit of the Lord pass from me to speak to you?" (1 Kings 22:24; NASB). He actually was deceived into believing that he was speaking by "the Spirit of the Lord" and that he was a true prophet of the Lord.

The situation is described by Micaiah. "Therefore, hear the word of the Lord. I saw the Lord sitting on His throne, and all the host of heaven standing by Him on His right and on His left" (1 Kings 22:19; NASB). This scene evidently depicts the whole realm of the supernatural, both good and bad. Micaiah continued:

> "And the Lord said, 'Who will entice Ahab to go up and fall at Ramoth-gilead?' And one said this while another said that.
> "Then a spirit came forward and stood before the Lord and said, 'I will entice him.'
> "And the Lord said to him, 'How?' And he said, 'I will go out and be a deceiving spirit in the mouth of all his prophets.' Then He said, 'You are to entice him and also prevail. Go and do so.'" (1 Kings 22:20-22; NASB)

Bluntly Micaiah informs Zedekiah, the servile prophet of Ahab, of the demonic nature and inevitable tragedy of the whole proceeding. "Now therefore, behold, the Lord has put a deceiving spirit in the mouth of all these your prophets; and the Lord has proclaimed disaster against you" (1 Kings 22:23; NASB).

The incident is a vivid illustration from the Old Testament of the New Testament revelation that demons inspire false prophets as well as give them their deceptive teachings and predictions. "Beloved, do not believe every spirit, but test the spirits to see whether they are from God; because *many false prophets* have gone out into the world" (1 John 4:1; NASB).

What a commentary is the deep demon deception of these prophets on the Spirit's explicit declaration that when believers "fall away from the faith" they pay "attention to deceitful spirits," with the result that they espouse "doctrines of demons" (1 Timothy 4:1; NASB), that is, teachings and predictions concocted and inspired by spirits not from God. "By means of the hypocrisy of liars," like Zedekiah and his fellow false prophets, these dupes of the devil become "seared in their own conscience as with a branding iron" (1 Timothy 4:2; NASB).

Blinded in false doctrine, trapped in doctrines of demons, and caught in some dangerous cult, their consciences become so cauterized and insensitive to light and truth that they not only believe a lie but also live it out daily. This is the fearful peril that faces every newly regenerated soul who is lured away from the Word of God and sound biblical teaching.

Satan and demons have their most astonishing success in the religious realm. They are especially eager to deceive believers and lead them into gross error of doctrine and conduct. The modern Babel of cults within the confines of professing Christianity is a standing witness to the devil's high bid for believers. Of course, many if not most of those entrapped are mere professors, not possessors, of saving faith. Yet the truth remains. Like at least some of Ahab's prophets of the Lord, all too many are truly regenerated believers.

And all too many of these have been influenced and invaded by spirits not from God in the religious realm—nice, goody-goody spirits whose one characteristic puts them in the demon class—they oppose the Word and will of God. This is not to mention those who have become bound by other spirits that are irreligious, blasphemous, sordid, and vile.

The dynamic that dominates all false teachers is "the spirit of uncleanness" (Zechariah 13:2; Hebrew text). This designation describes particularly the demons that operate in the area of religion and religious faith. Without doubt their role represents the most successful of all the demons' variegated activities. Here they defile the pure Word of God, despoil the people of God, and offer constant peril to the believer.

No spectacle is more tragic to see than a believer despoiled doctrinally by Satan, blinded by error, and brought under the delusion and enslavement of demonic teaching. Not until an attempt is made to rescue such a person from his predicament does one realize the powerful sway the demonic holds over the religiously enslaved believer.

It is my personal conviction that many of these cases represent severe demonization. The evil spirits are of the higher and finer variety, but they are still spirits "not from God" (1 John 4:1-3). Their more refined character blinds many persons to their real identity and the fact of their deep influence on the life and experience of the believer who has become invaded by them.

10

DEMONIZATION AND THE CHRISTIAN

Throughout this book the emphasis has been placed upon the fact that demonic power exerted upon a believer can be of various degrees of intensity. Stress has been laid upon the necessity of this fact because of the varying power, degree of wickedness, number, and actual control exercised by the spirits.

WHAT IS MEANT BY DEMONIZATION?

It has been demonstrated, moreover, that demonization (effecting the state of being demonized) is always brought about by demons who subject their victim to their control.[1] Demonization does *not* comprehend only affliction that is of a severe and enslaving nature. This latter type of severe demonization, however, is considered more in detail because the features latent in all instances of the phenomenon appear more saliently in it. In moderate and milder cases, some of these characteristics tend to lie hidden. Although latently present, they tend not to appear as readily as in the more enslaving cases.

DEMONIZATION IS MARKED BY DEMON CONTROL

The first fact that confronts us in demonization is that demons are in control of the demonized person. This is true of *all* degrees of demonization, including mild, moderate, and severe invasion. But in the severest cases the degree of control is much deeper and more domineering and enslaving. The number of demons may be higher, their wickedness greater, their strength more terrible, and their entrenchment in the life more binding. All of this is dramatically illustrated by the demonized man of Gadara (Mark 5:1-20; Luke 8:26-32). He was domineered by a legion of "demons" or "evil spirits," as both terms are applied to these denizens of the realm of evil supernaturalism (Mark 5:13; Luke 8:27).

A legion constituted the principal unit of the Roman army and consisted of from three thousand to six thousand foot soldiers with cavalry.[2] Suppose the term is used only metaphorically to denote a large military force or a very large number. It still reveals the amazing fact that this one man was controlled by a multitude of demons—enough, in fact, to madden a herd of two thousand hogs and cause them to rush down a hillside and be drowned in a lake.

Another enlightening feature of the demonic domination of this cruelly enslaved man was the fact that one of these evil spirits assumed control and evidently led the rest. This appears from Mark's account: "a man with an unclean spirit" met Jesus (Mark 5:2). This unclean spirit cried out of his victim and begged Jesus not to torment him by bidding him to leave (vv. 7-10). When Jesus demanded his name, he declared that it was "Legion." And the reason he gave was that "we are many" (v. 9), revealing that he was the leader and spokesman of the vast demon horde within.

Severely demonized people often have many demons controlling them. All these demons have names, and their names can be demanded by an accredited representative of Jesus, as Jesus Himself demanded them. The evil spirit can also be cast out of its victim by the use of its *name* by the accredited representative of Jesus, as Jesus Himself did.

This phenomenon did not occur only in Jesus' day. It is a common procedure today where prayer battles are conducted for the release of the demonized. I can personally attest, as the witness of similar releases, how important it is to confront the demon *by name*. He may answer back, but he is subject to Christ's servants and must go to the abyss (Luke 8:31) under Christ's authority and on the basis of the *position in Christ* of the one afflicted. I have witnessed numbers of such demons come out of their victims *by name* with horrible noises.

DEMONIZATION IS MARKED BY THE
INTRODUCTION OF A NEW PERSONALITY

This is the chief differentiating characteristic. The demon speaks out of the victim, frequently giving his name and where he has come from. The leader demon in the demoniac of Gadara cried out of his victim in another voice and as a conflicting personality: "What do I have to do with You, Jesus, Son of the Most High God? I implore You by God, do not torment me!" (Mark 5:7; NASB).

When our Lord demanded to know the demon's name, as already noted, the evil spirit replied, "My name is Legion: for we are many" (Mark 5:9). The demons also earnestly entreated Jesus not to send them into the abyss, the prison house of the demons (Luke 8:31; NASB).

In the use of pronouns, the first person always refers to the demon. The bystanders are addressed in the second person, while the victim is usually referred to in the third person. In the demonized state, when the spirit takes control, the demonized is in an unconscious state. His personality is eclipsed while the demon personality takes over. The new personality manifests itself in facial expressions, physical manifestations, feelings, and statements that belong to it, not to the temporarily eclipsed personality of the victim.

A similar phenomenon occurs in psychiatry, where a mental disorder results in a division or separation of the functions of the mind. But in demonization an evil spirit personality temporarily eclipses the normal personality.

In the case of the Gadarene, on the one hand, he runs to Jesus, apparently for help. On the other hand, he reacts in fear and begs Him not to torment him. There is an obvious visible and terrible conflict within the demonized person. He never knows from one moment to the next when the powers of darkness will choose to take over and black out his personality.

It is the ghastly circumstance of having squatters in your home, and you never know when they will decide to take over completely and do whatever they want in your house. Meanwhile, you do not know what they are doing, being at the time completely at their mercy and under their control.

The new interjected personality enables the severely demonized person to speak with voices that are not his own and in languages he has never studied. It is a common occurrence for a woman in the demonized state to speak with the deep bass of a man's voice or a man to speak with a woman's voice. It is not unusual for a severely demonized person to speak with many voices, for each demon may speak out by using the victim's tongue and vocal cords. But the amazing thing is that the new personality (or personalities, as the case may be) often speaks languages completely unknown to the victim. This was a very common phenomenon in nineteenth-century China.[3] In the famous case of Gottlieben Dittus, the demons who were finally disentrenched from their victim through the ministry of Pastor Blumhardt "spoke in all the European languages and in some which Blumhardt and others did not recognize."[4]

To attempt to account for this phenomenon as a simple case of schizophrenia will not work. No mentally ill or hysterical person can suddenly begin speaking a real foreign tongue that he has never studied. Nor can he do this in a completely different personality.

DEMONIZATION IS MARKED BY SUPERHUMAN STRENGTH

In extreme cases of demonization, like the demoniac of Gadara, the display of strength through the demonized body is amazing because it is supernatural. Of Legion it is said, "No one was able to bind him any more, even with a chain; because he had often been bound with shackles and chains, and the chains had been torn apart by him and the shackles broken in pieces, and no one was strong enough to subdue him" (Mark 5:3-4; NASB).

Luke relates that "the unclean spirit . . . had seized him [its victim] many times; and he was bound with chains and shackles and kept under guard; and yet he would burst his fetters and be driven by the demon into the desert" (Luke 8:29; NASB).

This is the explanation of at least some of the cases of horrible violence today, of people going berserk, of supernatural rage and the need for padded cells. Cases of mild or moderate demonization do not exhibit this phenomenon. It occurs only in instances where particularly vicious demons, often in large numbers, become deeply entrenched. The narratives of the demonized man of Gadara indicate that he had become progressively worse. Evidently he had already plumbed "the depths of Satan" (cf. Revelation 2:24) when he encountered Jesus and was wonderfully delivered.

Another biblical instance of superhuman strength exhibited by the chronically demonized is found in the demoniac at Ephesus who turned on the seven sons of the Jewish chief priest when they attempted to cast out demons in the name of Jesus, whom Paul preached: "The man, in whom was the evil spirit, leaped on them and subdued . . . and overpowered them, so that they fled out of that house naked and wounded" (Acts 19:16; NASB).

Counselors and workers with the demonized frequently encounter this phenomenon. Kurt Koch tells of a frail young man in the Philippines who was severely demonized. "When the supernatural rage struck him, he sometimes needed nine grown men to hold him down."[5] Cases of this superhuman display of strength in the demonized state are common in the literature on the subject.[6] Some of these are as remarkable, if not more so, than the account of the demoniac of Gadara in the Bible.[7]

I have personally observed such a display of violent strength. It occurred during a prayer session of Christians for a young convert who was severely tormented by many demonic powers. While in the unconscious demonized state, when the demons were manifest and in control, suddenly he leaped up from the pallet on which he was reclining and seized a heavy piece of furniture. Brandishing it in midair, he threatened to hurl it at those engaged in battle for his release. Doubtless he would have thrown the object had the demon energizing him not been rebuked and forced to leave its victim.

Other physical symptoms often appear in cases of chronic demonization, such as facial and body contortions, suicidal mania, extreme fear, immorality, and abrupt changes in ethical values. Sometimes demonization may take the form of physical illness, as in the cases of the woman with "a spirit of infirmity" (Luke 13:11-16) and the epileptic boy who had physical symptoms that were due to a demon (Matthew 17:14-18). Sometimes deafness (Mark 9:25), dumbness (Matthew 9:32-33), and even blindness (Matthew 12:22) had their causes not in the natural but in the demonic.

DEMONIZATION IS MARKED BY
AVERSION TO THE THINGS OF GOD

The invading demonic power manifests itself in a deep-rooted resistance to anything godly or spiritual. The demons "believe" that God is one "and shudder" (James 2:10; NASB), but they do not submit to Him or own His lordship over them.

The unclean spirit, the leader and spokesman of all the other demons that infested the demoniac of Gadara, "cried out with a loud voice" before Jesus and said, "What do I have to do with You, Jesus, Son of the Most High God?" (Mark 5:7; NASB). The evil spirit knew who Jesus was. He realized that He was Lord of the spirit world, but his attitude was that of deep resentment and opposition.

This extreme hostility toward spiritual things is common to all severely demonized people. The demon that troubled King Saul could not stand the sweet spiritual music of young David and left its victim when the musician performed in the monarch's presence (1 Samuel 16:23).

Prayer in the name of Jesus, reading and claiming promises of Scripture, and singing hymns of praise to God are sure means to rout demonic powers and secure the release of the victim. In fact, this is the simple order of deliverance sessions conducted by believers today who cultivate a humble, quiet ministry for God in this needy area.

DEMONIZATION IS MARKED BY CLAIRVOYANCE

The invading demon has supernatural power to discern things not naturally discernible to the senses. The Gadarene knew who Jesus was immediately, as soon as he saw him, although they had never met before. He recognized, too, that Jesus was the Son of the Most High God and had the power to deliver him by expelling the demons (Mark 5:6-7).

People in various stages of demonization give evidence of knowledge and intellectual powers not normally or naturally possessed by the victim. This is not a natural gift; it is the superhuman knowledge of the demon being manifested through its victim.

Clairvoyance is common in all stages of demonization. It occurs even among Christian faith healers who have mediumistic abilities that become the vehicle for spirits not from God to operate under the guise of the Holy Spirit. Such clairvoyants are able to sense who is ill and what their illness is, and to be used as a medium of healing.

DEMONIZATION IS SUBJECT TO INSTANT CURE

As Lord of the spirit world, Christ had absolute power over the demons. At His word they instantly left the demonized man and entered a herd of two thousand swine. In a moment the demoniac was completely delivered. Those who came to the scene were amazed and frightened to see him "sitting down, clothed and in his right mind, the very man who had had the legion" (Mark 5:15; NASB).

What a contrast this is to the long and tedious treatment of the insane so well known to psychiatry. For such phenomena, the psychiatric world, operating in the purely natural realm, has no valid answer.

But deliverances today normally take time. Often in severe cases, protracted prayer battles are necessary before complete expulsion of all demons takes place. A young Christian I know, who was severely demonized, has been the object of prayer in numerous deliverance sessions. Jesus Christ, as Lord of the spirit world, could evict these foul spirits with a word, instantly. It may take more time with His finite, infirm servants, but victory is *always* certain in His name.

DEMONIZATION IS MARKED BY THE PHENOMENON OF TRANSFERENCE

Demons in a demonized person may be transferred to other persons, animals, or, apparently in some cases, relegated to the abyss, the prison of the demons (Luke 8:31; NASB; cf. Revelation 9:1-12). The transference of the legion of demons from the demoniac to the herd of two thousand swine, which went berserk and rushed headlong into the lake, constitutes another feature of demonization that distinguishes it from mental illness. Events like this are just not accounted for in the field of medicine and psychiatry.

An evangelical pastor in Switzerland was reared in a family that practiced witchcraft and sorcery. His father was an active spiritist and magician. As an unsaved boy, he was demonized. However, when an evangelist came to their village, both he and his father were soundly converted. Immediately after the father and son became believers, the pigs in a nearby pigpen started to squeal and in a frenzy began to rush around madly. After a period of five hours, when nothing availed to calm them down, the farmer was compelled to shoot all of them. The converted son later entered a seminary and became a pastor.

CAN A BELIEVER BECOME DEMONIZED?

Having surveyed exactly the marks of extreme demonization, it is necessary to inquire whether a truly regenerated person could ever be so slavishly dominated by demon powers. The Gadarene, of course, was not a believer. Moreover, he evidently represents demonization in its most frightfully severe degree. Imagine thousands of demons in one man— enough to frenzy two thousand pigs! Purposely the Spirit of God selected this acute case to highlight the glorious power of Christ, the Savior, over the spirit world and to show how the powers of darkness can dominate lost humanity. A severely chronic case accentuates the characteristics of all other cases in the same general category, but its severity must not be allowed to color milder cases.

In considering the possibility of a true believer being severely demonized, it seems unthinkable that he would ever become possessed to the extent of the demoniac of Gadara. Yet, one might pause to ask what would have happened if the delivered man had reverted back to the sins of his old life. Could he have been demonized again? If so, could he ever have returned to the degree he had sunk to before he was saved?

But in considering such an eventuality we are dealing with what seems to be a purely hypothetical case in so-called Christian lands (that are fast becoming anything but "Christian" because of the frightening secularistic trend in contemporary society). But think of the condition that prevails in pagan cultures. There, when a person is saved out of centuries of entrenched paganism and demon-ridden occultism, he runs a grave risk, if he does not separate himself from witchcraft and sin, of being demonized again.

This has been the testimony of many veteran evangelical missionaries who have faced the dark demon world of pagan idolatry. It is also the opinion of Christian preachers and counselors who have had experience with people saved out of paganism in demon-ridden countries. It is also true in America today, as in the case of Beverly, the demonized Christian girl whose experience we related in chapter 5.

Clinical evidence abounds that a Christian can be demon-controlled as a carryover from preconversion days or can fall under Satan's power after conversion and became progressively demonized, even seriously. If such a person blatantly lives in scandalous sin, subscribes to and embraces heresy, engages in occultism, or gives himself to rebellion and lawlessness against God's Word and will, he may expect a demon invasion of his life.

A CASE IN POINT

Pat had been a believer for about a year. He was a student in a Bible college in the Philippines. He had confessed his sins and received forgiveness and the assurance of salvation. Yet, he had not yielded his life completely to God's will. In addition to this, he came from a family that had a history of occult oppression because his mother had been a practicing sorceress. These two circumstances seem to be the determining factors in Pat's becoming demonized.

Suddenly one day he complained of a terrible headache and nausea and went to the director of the school to ask him to pray for him. While the director was praying, the student suddenly lost consciousness and went into the demonized state. He became so violent that it took several men to hold him down. Strange voices began to speak out of his mouth.

One of the faculty members present addressed these voices: "In the name of the Lord Jesus, tell us why you have invaded Pat."

"Because he did not surrender his life completely," the voices responded.

"How many are you?" continued the interrogators.

"Fifty" came the reply.

Several of the faculty continued to counsel with the young man. They commanded the demons to leave him alone. All this was a call to a real spiritual battle that was to last a total of nineteen and a half hours until complete victory was won and all fifty demons had been expelled. Various faculty members and students joined in the conflict.

At one phase of the struggle one of the teachers commanded the demon voices to tell their names. One voice identified itself as Rakrek from Manchuria. Asked why they had come to the school, they boldly asserted, "To bring in modernism and liberalism."

When a faculty member heard that the voice had come from Manchuria, he recited a Russian verse he knew. The entire company witnessed a surprising thing. The voice at once began to speak in fluent Russian. Pat himself knew only English and his local Filipino dialect.

In the course of the fierce struggle, one of the demons boldly declared, "We have come to destroy Pat." Instantly the young man tried desperately to choke himself. His strength was such that he had to be restrained with force. Sometimes six and as many as nine men were required to hold him down to keep him from killing himself.

When the Russian demon declared that a group of Communists in Manila were planning to do away with Pat, a psychiatrist who was present notified the police. Also present to assist in the struggle were a Christian psychiatrist and a Christian psychologist, both of whom were absolutely convinced that Pat was demonized and not ill.

It turned out that the fifty demons were from all over the world—Russia, Tibet, Egypt, Sumatra, Holland. This partly explains the various languages they spoke. All of them were dominated by fear of the name and the coming of the Lord.

After the long struggle, Pat was completely set free. When the last demon was ousted, Pat regained consciousness. At first he began to cry, and then he started to praise the Lord. During all this titanic spiritual battle, Pat knew nothing of what happened. It was only after the prayer warriors had told him that he realized what had actually taken place. This overwhelming experience caused all the teachers and students present to join in repentance, prayer, and rededication to God's will as they placed themselves afresh under the protection of Christ's atoning blood.[8]

LESS SEVERE BUT MORE COMMON CASES OF DEMONIZATION

In less severe cases of demonization the resident demons hide themselves more cleverly from detection, and the new personality introduced merges more imperceptibly with the victim's own personality. Moreover, the paroxysm and trancelike state of actual demonization may occur only if the demons are challenged with expulsion.

In fact, it is usually only when the demons are about to be driven out that they discard their disguise and audibly give vent to their fears and horror of eviction, sometimes with an incoherent mumbling, sometimes with an eardrum-splitting yell. I personally have heard them yawn wearily and declare, "We are tired. Leave us alone." Others parody gospel hymns, singing, "Oh how I hate Jesus."

L. W. Elford, a missionary to the pagan Cree people of northern Saskatchewan, Canada, tells of an experience with a fellow missionary. Elford relates that God in His mercy had done a sanctifying and cleansing work in his own heart and had given him facility in using the Word of God as the sword of the Spirit against the adversary.

In the summer of 1965 he was taking a trip by water with two other missionaries when, one evening, one of his companions confessed that he was in bondage to a certain sin. So awful was its grip on him that he said, "There can be no deliverance." His two missionary colleagues told him they would pray for him. They did so that evening as they camped on the riverbank.

As Elford began to pray, a strange cry issued from the victim's lips. Then he was immobile and silent, except for incoherent mumbling. Meanwhile, the two praying missionaries were acutely aware of an overpowering evil spirit presence, and the afflicted missionary lost consciousness and lapsed into the demonized state.

The prayer warriors resisted this for what seemed to be two hours or more. Then, all of a sudden, the afflicted missionary regained consciousness and related the following story:

"When you began praying for me, everything turned black. I began vomiting words out. I could hear these words. But it was not I who was talking. I also could hear you praying as if at a distance."

The demon-afflicted believer was set completely free that day. When Elford saw him ten years later, he was a happy, radiant Christian.[9]

Another interesting example of the demonization of a believer comes from the Philippines and is told by missionary Ron Esson.[10] It occurred at the annual conference of the Palawan Association of Baptist Churches held at Puerto Princesa. The believer was a young man who on the first day of the conference was attacked by demon powers. He was unconscious and lying on a bamboo bed. Efforts to arouse him were futile.

Clutching his Bible tightly to his breast, he was writhing back and forth and whimpering pitiably. He had no fever and gave no indication of any definite physical sickness. But his whole condition bore unmistakable evidence of demon molestation of a believer, which Ron Esson says he had witnessed in Mindanao some years previously.

The believers all gathered around the young man's bed to sing and pray. As the third person was praying, the young man's eyes fluttered open.

"Thank the Lord for freeing you!" cried the missionary.

"Praise the Lord!" he responded, visibly relaxing. Soon he was able to sit up and take some nourishment. Then he related that three spirit beings, masquerading as seductive young women, had appeared to him, tempting him. This was not the first time they had tried to seduce him. He had had this experience before at his home.

The spirits also had been trying to snatch his Bible from him. All who witnessed the struggle saw the Bible move as though it was being violently pulled out of his hands. Actually, he had to clutch it desperately to hold onto it.

When he was questioned concerning how this all began, he was quite reticent and vague in his answers. But it is certain that there was some inlet in his own life or in his background that opened the door to invasion by evil spirits. Whatever the reason, the Lord wonderfully released him to a normal, happy Christian life.

THE CASE OF A CONVERTED WIFE OF A WITCH DOCTOR

Judith Bartel, a missionary to Colombia, relates the remarkable story of the postconversion struggle with demons of Marina, the converted wife of a witch doctor in the Ubate area, where witchcraft is widely practiced.[11]

Before she and her husband were saved, Marina was the medium through which her spiritist spouse could communicate with the spirits. It soon became apparent that, although Marina was genuinely saved, the demon grip on her life had not been completely broken.

Having a large house, the converted spiritists opened it to the believers. It was while the Christians were having devotions the next day that Marina went into a trance and began babbling. It was soon evident that it was not Marina speaking, but a demon spirit speaking through her. The believers demanded that the demon tell his name. He said he was the demon of asthma and had been resident for eighteen years.

As the believers were praying in Spanish, Marina rose from the floor, where she had been writhing horribly, and screamed at Judith Bartel in an unintelligible language. But suddenly the demon in her screamed at the missionary in English.

"Never, never, I will never leave her body! Her body is mine! Never, never!"

The believers urged Marina to plead the name of Jesus and claim the power of his blood. But the demon had paralyzed her vocal cords, and she was speechless. After about an hour's prayer struggle, Marina began to convulse on the floor. With a bloodcurdling yell the demon released her, wrenching and contorting her body fearfully.

But the battle was far from over. After the service on Friday evening, the believers were praying for Marina's husband, Enrique, who had a terrible back pain. It was during this prayer time that Marina again lapsed into the demonized state. This time the spirit that took over declared that his name was Ismael, a Bogota witch doctor whom the evil spirit impersonated. He convulsed Marina's unconscious body and declared that she belonged to him.

Only by prayer and singing hymns was this powerful demon evicted. Marina then regained consciousness. She remembered that four years or so previously she had visited a witch doctor in Bogota, but she had forgotten his name and address.

Up to this point there was some doubt in Judith Bartel's mind whether what was operating in this woman was not some mental trauma or psychological abnormality of some sort. But the experience that followed on Sunday night dispelled all doubt that they were fighting against the spirit powers of darkness (Ephesians 6:10-20).

After the Sunday night service, the group of believers decided to have devotions before retiring. Marina was present, but there was no indication of anything unusual. During the prayer that followed, Marina's Bible fell from her hands, and she suddenly rolled over unconscious in the demonized state.

Again another demon spoke from her. Marina fastened her eyes on the missionary with a look of horrible evil. Involuntarily the missionary cried out, "You can't touch me. I'm covered by the blood of Christ!"

All those present claimed Christ's blood as the terrible gaze of the demon working through Marina fell on each of them. Then ensued a terrific attack in which Marina's body was cruelly convulsed. During this agony, Marina's consciousness returned, and she began to cry out that the spirit was back in her body and that she was being choked to death. She was urged to claim the blood of Christ, but she said she could not. All she could do was scream over and over again, "My God, my God, my God!"

Then a strange thing happened. Marina's husband was present and suddenly his wedding ring fell off and hit the floor. One of the believers picked it up and handed it back to him. They then asked him, because he was such a new convert, to leave the room and pray elsewhere.

What followed was so horrible that the believers thought that Marina would perish from suffocation. Her screams and groans were terrifying as she changed color from lack of oxygen.

As the believers were taking Marina out into a car to rush her to the hospital, the missionary went into the house to care for Marina's five-month-old baby who was to a degree sharing the same experience as the mother. Suddenly the baby relaxed in the missionary's arms. At the same instant outside on the street, Marina screamed in Spanish, "Glory to God! Yes, there's power in the blood of Jesus!"

She had been delivered instantly. A Christian physician, Dr. Pinio, who was to take her to the hospital, told what had happened. As they were about to leave for the hospital, with Marina struggling for air, she asked them to take off her wedding ring since it was very tight. Dr. Pinio forced off the ring, and, as it fell into his hands, he screamed. A bolt of electricity passed through his body, and the ring fell to the floor, bouncing as if it had a life of its own.

As Dr. Pinio screamed, Marina also screamed, for her release was immediate. Her husband immediately took off his ring, saying he didn't know why it had fallen off shortly before, but he felt there was some binding power in those rings. For some bizarre reason the demons had a foothold because of the rings. Perhaps the marriage it sealed was viewed by Satan as binding since the husband as a spiritist was able to contact the spirits through his wife who was the actual medium. Satan did not relinquish this useful team of his without a struggle.

The whole episode is a red-flag warning of the utter peril of occultism. Believers can be demonized as a carryover from the old life, before they were saved, particularly when they were immersed in spiritism. Believers also may become demonized if they go back to practicing the same sins, particularly occultism, out of which they were saved.

A COLLEGE STUDENT DELIVERED FROM DEMONIC SHACKLES

I first came in contact with Vincent one evening in January 1975. He called me long-distance from Michigan. A young man in his early twenties, during his college years he had developed very serious physical, emotional, and mental problems.

So severe had his condition become that he had had to drop out of the University of Michigan, where he had been enrolled in science courses preparatory to a premedical degree. He was unable to study because of his utter inability to concentrate. His mental and emotional faculties had been reduced to complete chaos.

Vince had become heavily involved in drugs—acid, marijuana, and other narcotics—and was high most of the time. He had undergone extensive psychiatric treatment both at the University Psychological Clinic in Ann Arbor and also under a private hypnotherapist and psychiatrist. Both individual and group therapy were tried without positive results. All this treatment, however good it was, did not seem to touch his problem.

In fact, Vince's condition grew worse and became almost intolerable. He described his head as being detached from his body, so that he had no control over his thinking pattern. In group therapy, when he was asked what his goals were, Vince's reply was "to have my head back on my shoulders."

Strange voices plagued his inner consciousness and accused him constantly on the ground of "the sins of his youth." His wide reading in psychology seemed only to add to his confusion. Tension, depression, anxiety, and hopelessness overwhelmed him. His one obsession became a desire to do away with himself. Miraculously, he had not acted on his suicidal impulses.

Although he had been baptized into the Roman Catholic church, the faith his Italian ancestors had embraced for generations, Vince had drifted away from Catholicism after his confirmation. Although his mother was a devout Catholic and his father merely a nominal professor, Vince clashed with them, not so much because he had left the church, but because of his erratic behavior and apparent failure to face life.

Through a friend, the son of a minister, Vince began attending a Bible-preaching church in Detroit, where he faced the claims of the gospel. For the first time he began to perceive that whatever his problem was, God had the answer. He therefore began to seek help in prayer. But in the prayer session, when he lasped into a comalike state of uncon-sciousness and strange noises and blasphemies began to come from his mouth, the pastor, his assistant, and several other Christians did not know enough of the working of de-monic powers to enable them to diagnose the case clearly and pursue a plan of deliverance intelligently.

It was while Vince was in the pastor's study one day that he was irresistibly directed to pull a copy of my book *Demons in the World Today* off the shelf.[12] As he began reading about the operation of demons in human personality, his problem began to be seen in focus. It was at this juncture that my telephone rang. Vince was calling from Detroit, and he arranged with me to fly to my home in Maryland to discuss his problem.

Concluding that his trouble was definitely demonic, I advised him that, as a child of God, he could seek and obtain full emancipation from the sinister spirits that had invaded him and that were tormenting him and deranging him men-tally and emotionally.

I cautioned him, however, that the difficulty was acute and would take time. He was to return to Detroit and seek out a small prayer group that would understand his plight and undertake a protracted prayer struggle for his release. Unfor-tunately, I knew of no such prayer group in Detroit at the moment.

But God was leading both Vince to be delivered and me to aid in his deliverance. While conducting a Bible confer-ence we learned of a woman who had had extensive experi-ence and a blessed ministry in praying for demon-enslaved people. A tried and tested servant of the Lord, she was ap-proaching her eightieth birthday.

As soon as I met her and heard of her prayer group, I wrote to Vince in Detroit, telling him about the Lord's lead-ing. At the time when the letter arrived, Vince said he was hopelessly disheartened.

My news fired Vince's soul with new hope and anticipation. He sensed almost immediately that the Lord was directing him to go to see this woman. But no sooner had Vince decided to seek help from this woman and her prayer group than he became so ill physically that he had to be hospitalized. Strangely, every conceivable test turned out negative. The doctors could find no natural cause for what they had first thought was typhoid fever. The attack appeared to be nothing more than a bold demonic onslaught to keep Vince from going. But the Holy Spirit so blessed Vince that even in the worst phase of the sickness he was able to pray and to be joyfully assured of recovery. Soon he was well and aboard a plane.

What transpired is so incredible that many will not believe it. Perhaps I might be skeptical myself if I had not heard it with my own ears via tapes. These tapes recorded six of the prayer sessions this woman and her prayer helpers conducted during the fall of 1975 for Vince's release from a severe state of demonization.

The first important thing to remember about these various sessions is that they were called and conducted with *one* purpose in mind: to confront and dislodge the demonic spirits. These warriors had this *one* aim in their prayer, praise, and Scripture reading. They entered the battle (and a battle it is!) to ferret out the foe, dislodge him, and cast him into the pit—the abyss or prison of the demons (Luke 8:31).

That is why, according to the tapes, the battle in these sessions normally ensues immediately. Vince prayed, read, and claimed a portion of Scripture, gave his testimony of his position of blessing in Christ, and enunciated emphatically his firm stand against the invading demon hordes. But then, as soon as the workers started dealing with the demons, the demons "knocked their victim out."

What happened from this point on was a conflict between the workers and the demonic powers. The only exception occurred when for any reason the prayer partners called the afflicted one back from the demonized state of uncon-sciousness in which the demonic powers act and speak through their victim. The workers would do this sometimes once or more during the course of an hour's prayer battle.

As soon as Vince would be "knocked out by the de-mons" (to use their graphic expression for lapsing into the demonized state), the group would always accost these evil spirits with incisive directness and demand that they tell their names. All the demons have names, but frequently a struggle ensues to get the demon spirit to identify himself. But this is of utmost importance.

Once the demon is identified by name and is faced, he is mercilessly grilled and engaged, as it were, in hand-to-hand encounter, much like two men fighting a duel. The worker fights with "the sword of the Spirit," the Word of God. The demon counters with "the fiery darts of the wicked [one]" (Ephesians 6:16).

The Christian soldier seeks by each thrust of the sword to dislodge and rout the demon by the Word of God. In one of these sessions when the demon was contacted, the woman demanded, "Give your name!" The demon did so, but only after dogged persistence. The spirit gave his name as "Lust."

"Every one of you demons of lust, get out. Go to the pit!"

"We'll not go!" the demon retorted.

"Vince is a child of God. He is washed in the blood of Christ!" persisted the woman.

"We'll kill him!" screamed an enraged demon, cursing the blood of Christ.

In this particular session the demons of lust that were confronted were so blasphemous, vile, and stubborn that the workers called Vince back from his unconscious state to re-nounce any ground he may have given to the sinister spirits and to take a fresh firm stand on the Word of God against them.

Then, as Vince lapsed back into the demonized state, the workers prayed and claimed anew the power of the Word of God and position in Christ. With that, there were horrible coughings and writhings of Vince's body as a number of demons of lust left in quick succession.

There had been times during some of the sessions, particularly when dealing with demons of "violence" and "rebellion," when Vince became violent and very strong while in the unconscious demonized state. Suddenly he would dart up from off the pallet on which he normally reclined during the prayer battles like a spurt of water from a fountain. In a split second he would seize a heavy piece of furniture to hurl at one of the workers.

However, no one was ever hurt by the demons. It is remarkable how subject they were to the workers (Matthew 10:1; Luke 10:17). A simple command given in the name of Jesus Christ controlled Vince (rather, the demon power acting through him).

If the woman commanded a demon to quote a Scripture or declare a truth, the demon sometimes balked or refused or deliberately misquoted the Scripture or distorted the truth. However, she and her co-laborers kept dunning the demon until he was forced, not only to say it, but to say it correctly.

For example, she would say to the demon, "Christ is Victor." Repeat, "Christ is Victor!"

"Satan is victor," the demon retorted.

But the evil spirit was not let off the hook. He *had* to declare, "Christ is Victor," and when he did, he was forthwith expelled.

Those who have witnessed these spiritual conflicts can attest to the fact that once the demon is identified and engaged in actual conflict, the situation is like a person embroiled in a fight. It is never easy to get out of it, and sometimes it is impossible.

Normally, if the warrior who engages him is "strong in the Lord" (Ephesians 6:10) and persistent in faith, the demon is vanquished and dislodged from his victim on the spot.

One of the striking features of the sessions with Vince was the large numbers of demons confronted, identified, and expelled. I was sent a list of these spirits expelled by name between the last week in June and the second week in November 1975.

The list contained more than sixty-five demons of the mind. Vince's mind had been in a state of chaotic disorientation. It is not surprising that the demons identified themselves with names such as Depression, Amnesia, Fatigue, Filthy Fantasies, Fragmented Thought, Illusory (visions/voices), Psychic Disturbance, and Nervous Disorder.

The list contained almost as many demons of the emotions (operating on the feelings) as of the mind. They had names such as Sadness, Sorrow, False Happiness, Fear, Impatience, Hate, Anger, Anxiety, Insecurity, and Loneliness. Also included were the names of demons that work more directly through the body, such as Sexual Perversion, Sodomy, Homosexuality, and Pornography.

At another session, when Vince was in the demonized state, lying on the pallet, the demons were viciously vile and blasphemous. So the woman summoned Vince from his unconscious state and asked him to renounce any ground that the demons might have taken to be so bold. Vince prayed movingly and recited and claimed Revelation 12:11: "And they overcame him by the blood of the Lamb, and by the word of their testimony."

As he sank back on the pallet to return to the demonized state, the demons began to leave one by one with unearthly screams and moans. It was one of the most rewarding sessions.

"We're too weak to fight back," one demon groaned. Another, as if expiring from sheer fatigue, wearily gasped, "Whew!"

Other astonishing characteristics of the demons that were confronted in Vince (besides their number, hostility, and blasphemy) were their accusations and bold threats. When the Christian workers undertook to command them to repeat, "Jesus Christ is Vincent's Lord," the reply was *"Satan is Vincent's Lord."* Only by the dogged persistence of the workers did the demons repeat, "Jesus Christ is Vincent's Lord."

At one session they yelled defiantly, "We're going to smash his [Vince's] car and kill him!" This threat to kill their victim was uttered a number of times at various sessions. At another session they cried, "We'll break his leg!" On another occasion, when Vince was in the state of coma, they declared, "We are not going to let him come back. We're going to choke him to death!" Several times they turned on the woman or one of her assistants and, through the use of their victim's vocal cords, yelled, "We'll kill you!"

At one point, when the woman insisted, "Christ died for Vincent on the cross," they cried derisively, "What cross? There's no such thing as the cross. It's a big fairy tale." One demon with a high piercing voice yelled, "Christ died for everybody else, but *not* for Vincent." Some of the demons emptily boasted, "We were at the cross and tried to kill Jesus." When the elect unfallen angels were mentioned, they hissed scornfully, "A bunch of sissies!" When the demons were asked, "Who defeated you?" they cried, "Judas!"

She wrote me, "The language of the demons is often profane and vile. But Vince is *always* completely unaware of what they are saying. The stark contrast between what *they* say and what *he* says adds greatly to the reality of the situation. We always praise God for Vince's true expression of his faith, the sincerity expressed in his prayers, and the stand he takes in Christ against these invading powers."

Many people ask why, in some instances, it takes so long to realize full deliverance. This woman, who is a veteran in this ministry, wrote me concerning this question. I can do no better than quote from her letter: "I know the Lord *could* cast them all out at once. But I do not believe that is His will.

These people *grow* in the Lord, as they take His victory day by day. They recognize the heinousness of sin, face the powers of the enemy, realize that they themselves cannot fight the battle. Through this they really learn to cry in faith to the Lord in their dire need. They learn the necessity of constantly abiding in Christ and living on His every word. By the time deliverance is completed, they are walking steadily in victory, fully desiring to serve the Lord faithfully."

WHY DELIVERANCE SOMETIMES TAKES SO LONG: A TESTIMONY

Often deliverance from demon power is such a protracted struggle that many fainthearted believers become discouraged. The following testimony was sent to me from a woman in Florida who found salvation and subsequent emancipation from demon harassment and offers her conviction as to why the Lord did not deliver her all at once:

Although the testimony which I want to share is not as dramatic as some, I am writing to you because of the specific nature of it.

The details leading up to my regeneration are too time-consuming to relate, but after many years of hearing the Gospel, living under a false sense of security in believing that I had received Christ, I was driven by a shocking and unexpected chain of events to think that I had committed the unpardonable sin.

I acquired the name of Mrs. F M. She explained the *true* gospel to me, and the Lord showed me that I had never seen myself worthy of hell, that I had sinned primarily against God, that I had had a sorrow for sin which was not true repentance, that old things never had passed away, that I was dead in trespasses and sins, and that the Lord Jesus Christ's substitutionary death on the cross was my only hope, by faith, of salvation.

The Lord mercifully saved me, and from that point showed me that I needed deliverance from demons. During the past two and one half years this process has continued. In the initial stages I expected total deliverance at each session. After several months, however, I began to realize that I was not strong enough in the Lord, schooled in His Word, nor grounded and settled in the faith to be able to stand "strong in the Lord and in the power of his might" against such powerful opposition of demonic forces. I read Exodus 23:28-30: "And I will send hornets before thee, which shall drive out the Hivite, the Canaanite, and the Hittite, from before thee. I will not drive them out from before thee in one year; lest the land become desolate, and the beast of the field multiply against thee. By little and little I will drive them out from before thee, until thou be increased, and inherit the land." This passage often has spoken to and comforted my heart.

Had I been delivered without knowing how to recognize and refuse the lies to which I had been enslaved for years, I believe I soon would have been re-invaded. Also, I would not have learned from an early deliverance the extent of my bondage and how far down the Lord had to reach to bring me up from the horrible pit, the miry clay, nor would I have been as aware as I now am of the rebellion of my own natural heart and the venom of all satanic forces against God.

These are a few of the reasons why I believe a prolonged deliverance process has been necessary for and beneficial to me—not that I'm grateful for demons for I despise them and long to be like Christ—but I marvel at the sovereign purposes of God in His dealings with me, and I praise Him with all my heart for His mercy, love, and grace toward me.

A Somber Warning

Such a realistic facing of the issue of how far Satan and demons can go in the life and experience of a truly born-again believer is bound to stir up opposition in some quarters. But let us, as God's people, be careful that we do not listen to the evil one. He would blind us to the extent of his power and deceive us as to exactly how far he can go in the case of God's people when they sin blatantly and scandalously.

Satan knows how far he can go. Let us be sure that we know as much as he knows on this score if we hope to get the better of him in the gigantic battle that is looming as the occult age advances and the demonic era, foretold in the end time, closes upon us like a thick fog.

Certainly Satan would like us to underestimate what he can do and how far he can go. How delighted he is to have us theorize in a theological dream world that does not face the relevant Scriptures fully and fairly nor come to grips with the facts of experience realistically. How gleeful he must feel if he can cast the halo of supposed orthodoxy over the whole procedure. He would like us to live in a fool's paradise so that we will be unable to sound a full warning to the perils of occult contanimation and other willful sins, as well as the demonic bondage that follows.

Surely we who reject the bugbear of the insecurity of the believer must honestly face the full issues of security and set forth fully *exactly* what the powers of darkness *can* do to seriously sinning saints. The results, far from doing harm, will do nothing but good. All sinners, including sinning saints, *must* be warned of the consequences of sin. Satan would not have it so. But let us, as God's people, *not* side with him on this momentous issue.

11

MEDIUMSHIP IN PIOUS MASQUERADE

As the end of the age draws near with its prophesied increase of satanic activity and deception, no Scripture sounds a more needed warning than that penned by the apostle Paul to the Corinthian believers: "And no wonder, for even Satan disguises himself as an angel of light. Therefore it is not surprising if his servants also disguise themselves as servants of righteousness; whose end shall be according to their deeds" (2 Corinthians 11:14-15; NASB).

This peril is facing the believer today as never before in the common phenomenon of occultism called mediumship. The real danger is not the manifestation of the phenomenon in occultism, where it belongs, but its pious masquerade under the Christian banner, where it most certainly does not belong and where it can work untold havoc.

Accentuating the hazard that faces multitudes of believers is their complete ignorance of the fact that pagan, satanic occult phenomena can don the false face of Christianity and appear as genuine gifts and manifestations of the Holy Spirit.

WHAT IS MEDIUMSHIP?

Mediumship is the condition of being or acting the role of a spiritualistic medium. A medium (from the Latin *medius*, neuter *medium*, meaning "middle") is a go-between or intermediary between the natural realm and the supernatural sphere of spirits. The adjective "mediumistic" means "relating to or having the abilities of a spiritualistic (spiritistic) medium."[1]

Mediumistic abilities and activities have no legitimate place in pure biblical Christianity. They fit into the category of darkness and have no claim to the light, for they are connected with Satan and demonic powers and have no place among gifts of the Spirit. They belong to Belial, not to Christ (2 Corinthians 6:14-18).

Mediumship is to be trenchantly differentiated from mediatorship. A mediator is a person who acts between two contending parties to reconcile them (Galatians 3:20). The term is applied to Moses, who came between the Lord and His people, as typical of Christ, the *one* and *only* Peacemaker between God and man (1 Timothy 2:5). In a limited sense, a believer is a mediator by virtue of his representing the *one* and *only* true Mediator to sinful man. But Scripture calls this role an ambassadorship (2 Corinthians 5:20) rather than a mediatorship.

On the other hand, a medium (psychic, clairvoyant, fortune teller, or witch) is in *no sense* an arbiter between God and man to reconcile them as two contending parties. He is purely a go-between or intermediary between the fallen angelic (demonic) creature (*not* the Creator) and fallen man. Moreover, there is no reconciliation of contending parties.

Mediumship is really an offshoot of idolatry. It follows, therefore, that it traffics in evil spirits who are opposed by the Word of God in severest terms (Leviticus 19:31; 20:27; Deuteronomy 18:10-11; 1 Samuel 28:3-25) because it constitutes a wicked affront to God and brazenly breaks the first two commandments of the eternal moral law of God reflected in the Mosaic Decalogue (Exodus 20:1-7).

God's people were "defiled" when they resorted to witches and wizards[2] who exercised mediumistic powers (Leviticus 19:31). God threatened to set His face against any believer who turned to such occultists to make use of their mediumistic abilities; he was to be "cut . . . off" from the Lord's people (Leviticus 20:6). Any believer who practiced mediumistic arts was to be stoned to death (Leviticus 20:27).

Although a believer is not a spiritistic medium, he can for one reason or another become contaminated with idolatry and spiritism, manifest mediumistic abilities, and become the vehicle for the operation of mediumistic powers. This is precisely where the peril lies and why in an era of growing occultism God's people must be instructed so as to be warned against mistaking mediumistic abilities for the genuine gifts of the Holy Spirit.

MEDIUMISTIC GIFTS

NATURAL AND SPIRITUAL GIFTS

At birth we are endowed with various powers and potentialities—physical, mental, emotional, and spiritual. These are in the category of natural endowments bestowed upon us by our Creator. Such natural gifts, for example, include bodily characteristics that have the potential for athletic achievement or prowess, mental abilities that presage a scholarly or inventive career, or artistic talents that make possible great success in the fields of the arts and the sciences.

At our second, or spiritual, birth we are endowed with *spiritual* gifts (Romans 12:3-8; Ephesians 4:7-16). These are the endowments of the Holy Spirit. When we are saved, the Spirit moves into our body and manifests Himself by working through our natural endowments and by equipping us with new abilities we never had before. These abilities enable the believer to glorify God in bringing God's blessings to man (1 Corinthians 12:7, 11).

Unsaved people, no matter how talented, have only natural gifts. Saved people, however, have both natural and supernatural gifts, since they have the Holy Spirit and a new nature through which the Holy Spirit works. But in their case, even their natural gifts become spiritual because the Holy Spirit uses them and makes them effective in Christian testimony and service.

Mediumistic gifts, however, are quite distinct from either natural gifts or the gifts of the Spirit. Natural gifts belong solely to the sphere of the natural. However, both spiritual gifts (gifts of the Holy Spirit) and mediumistic gifts (abilities exercised by spiritistic mediums) belong to the realm of the supernatural. The difference is that the former belong to the sphere of good supernaturalism while the latter belong to the sphere of evil supernaturalism.

THE SOURCE OF MEDIUMISTIC GIFTS

Genuine mediumistic gifts are demonic in character, although they may have begun in natural abilities that furnished the powers of darkness an open door of access. Extrasensory perception may in incipient stages be purely natural, as may be telepathy, mesmerism, and mental suggestion. But these extrasensory phenomena so easily become demonic that in cases where they are cultivated and not renounced they may become occult manifestations.

Scripture, in closely connecting mediumistic abilities with occultism and sorcery, shows them to be demonic and evil. Even scientific inquiry into these parapsychological phenomena runs the risk of demonic deception and enslavement.

The evil nature of mediumistic powers is further evidenced by the way they come into being. They originate in one of three ways: by heredity, occult participation, or occult transference.

Occult powers and mediumistic tendencies can be passed down from generation to generation. They run through the family tree of practicing sorcerers and magicians to the third and fourth generation of people implicated in idolatry and its inseparable companion, demonized religion

(Exodus 20:1-7; cf. 1 Corinthians 10:20). If a person's grand-parents were spiritists or mediums, he may expect his children, grandchildren, and even great-grandchildren to demonstrate mediumistic tendencies.

If a member of this occult line is saved, his mediumistic tendencies may at the same time vanish. But this is not always true. Often they remain. The believer, then, may possess mediumistic powers. He may not even know it because they are not under the control of the person's normal consciousness.

However, a believer, as he is taught the Word, can discover that he possesses these abilities, but also that he can and should be liberated as soon as possible from them because they are dangerous.

The tragedy in the case of some servants of God, who suddenly one day discover that they have these supernatural powers, is that they assume that these powers are from God. They mistakenly view them as some form of charismatic power especially given them to accomplish miracles of healing and other wonders after the pattern of the early apostolic church.

Mediumistic gifts can also be acquired through experimentation with occultism or occult religion. Participation in a séance, engaging in fortune-telling or magic, reading occult literature, or allowing oneself to be healed by occult powers can result in a person's becoming mediumistic.

Participation in occultism opens the personality to demonic invasion. This means that the invading demon power, which exploits natural endowments and psychic tendencies, will manifest itself in supernatural operations that very closely approximate the genuine gifts of the Spirit (cf. 1 Corinthians 12-14).

There are cogent reasons why all born-again people should steer clear of every form of occultism. This is especially true of the occult-contaminated forms of Christianity, which are becoming more widespread and dangerous in the occult age that has been developing with such frightful rapidity.

In addition, mediumistic gifts can develop as a result of occult transference. Strong magicians and sorcerers are able to impart their powers to others who desire them and will accept them. A dying witch or charmer can frequently transfer his occult powers to his children or to someone who will accept them. But transferred powers are never as strong as those inherited (passed on from generation to generation in one's family; cf. Exodus 20:1-6).

Of course, no contact should ever be had by a believer with a mediumistic practitioner. But in the case of believers, mediumistic abilities can always be gotten rid of and nullified through faith in Christ and prayer.

THE COUNTERFEIT NATURE OF MEDIUMISTIC GIFTS

Mediumistic gifts that imitate the gifts of the Holy Spirit are counterfeit. This observation alone should convince the believer of the great importance of knowing *exactly* what the Scriptures teach concerning these gifts so that he will be protected from the deception of falling prey to the counterfeit.

The earliest tabulation of spiritual gifts lists those that were operative in the early apostolic church about A.D. 57, when Christianity was being founded in a pagan world and before the New Testament Scriptures had come into existence. For this reason some of the nine gifts listed were "sign gifts"—those miraculously confirming the gospel message (Hebrews 2:4; 2 Corinthians 12:12)—like the gift of miracles, gifts of healings, the gift of tongues, and the interpretation of tongues. These sign gifts were not meant to be permanently operative once Christianity had become established.

Other gifts, such as the gift of prophecies, the gift of tongues, and the gift of knowledge (1 Corinthians 13:8-13), were *revelatory.* They were operative in the apostolic church because they were desperately needed for teaching purposes in the new church age until the New Testament should come into existence.

The gift of tongues fitted into both of these categories: sign gift and revelatory gift. As a revelatory gift, like the gift of prophecies and the gift of knowledge, it involved *direct revelation* by the Holy Spirit of truths now contained in the New Testament, but then available only by these temporary tideover gifts. When the tongue was *interpreted* it became revelatory, as with the gift of prophecies and the gift of knowledge.

God does perform miracles on occasion. But what shall we say of people who claim the gift of working miracles and healing the sick? This means a settled, permanent, Spirit-imparted ability to do these things.

The apostles had these gifts. But do we have apostles today? Do we need the sign gifts of an apostle now? Has not Christianity, like the infallible, inspired revelation upon which it was founded, been authenticated by miracle and fulfilled prophecy? Have not God's people for centuries walked by faith and not by sight (2 Corinthians 5:7)? Has that situation suddenly changed?

Unless the nature and purpose of these gifts in the apostolic church are clearly seen from the Word of God, do we not as God's people run a grave risk of mistaking mediumistic magic for miracles by the Holy Spirit? Is it not perilous to claim that *all* the gifts in the apostolic church should be exercised in the church today?

And what shall we say about the revelatory gifts that are definitely defined as temporary until the completed Scriptures became available for study and preaching (1 Corinthians 13:8-13)? Should we have the gift of prophecies in the church today? Remember that this means revelations of the future in addition to the written prophetic Word. If so, the visions of Emmanuel Swedenborg, Joseph Smith, and others may be in order. This means anyone can arise in the church with some new revelation purportedly from God. If it is not a new revelation, we do not need it. It is *already* contained in the written Word.

Should we have the gift of knowledge in the church today? Remember that this means *revelation of knowledge in addition to the written Word.* If it is not a new revelation, we repeat, we do not need it. If such knowledge is claimed, it moves into the province of the occult—the realm of the medium, the witch, the false prophet, and the fortune-teller.

This is a far cry from the holy domain where the Spirit has guided the inspired New Testament writers "into *all* the truth" and discloses to us "what is to come" in the future (John 16:13; NASB).

Should we have the gift of tongues in the church today? Remember, this means *revelation* of prophecies or knowledge *in addition to the written Word* given *indirectly* in another language, which has to be interpreted to be equivalent to the gift of prophecies or the gift of knowledge. If we gloss over the plain teaching of the Word of God, may we hope to escape deception through mediumistic counterfeit?

THE DEMONIC NATURE OF MEDIUMISTIC GIFTS

The demonic nature of mediumistic gifts is apparent, as we have already seen, from their close association with witchcraft and sorcery and their severe denunciation in Scripture. The demonic also appears in the evil way these counterfeit gifts originate through heredity in an occult-contaminated family line or through active participation in occultism or by transference from strongly occult-demoninated practitioners of witchcraft.

Further evidence of the demonic character of mediumistic powers appears in their close association with the pagan ritual of primitive tribes the world over. This is true whether of the so-called Hilot, the practicers of black magic in the Philippines, or of similar black-magic workers, called Kahunas, in the Hawaiian islands.

One of the Filipino Hilot chiefs, a magician by the name of Datu, was so demon-controlled that on occasion his hand would become so hot that an egg could be cooked upon it. When he was saved, he renounced the power because he realized that it was demonic. The tragedy is that many people in so-called Christian lands, which have become honeycombed with occultism, frequently mistake such mediumistic abilities for genuine spiritual gifts.

The so-called "hot hand" is not a new phenomenon among public faith healers. Kurt Trampler, a religious healer in Germany, displays his clairvoyant powers in accurately diagnosing sickness as Edgar Cayce used to do.[3] When Dr. Trampler brings his mediumistic powers to bear upon his patients, he inquires, "Do you feel a warmth coming over you?" The healing process is initiated by the clairvoyant diagnosis. It is followed by psychic mediumistic influencing.

But these mediumistic powers can be completely thwarted by sincere, earnest believers who desire only God's will and earnestly pray to God to that end. Neither Kurt Trampler nor any other healer can foist mediumistic healing upon anyone who thus honestly approaches God strictly on the basis of the revealed Word of God. In all such instances mediumistic healers without exception must confess that they cannot help.

The Hawaiian Kahunas can inflict disease on another person, even at a distance, by means of their mediumistic powers derived from the practice of black magic. Is this different from someone who leaves Christian Science and experiences persecution as a result of the negative use of mental suggestion? Mary Baker Eddy called it malpractice and described how it can be employed to magically persecute people one wishes to attack.

Whether it is a Kahuna or a malpracticing Christian Scientist, the dynamic behind it is the same. The only difference is that in Hawaii the power is demonstrably pagan. In so-called Christian lands, it masquerades under a Christian costume.

A somber fact must be faced by many naive Christians in the Western world. They must realize that all magic is sinful and must be renounced. It does not make any difference whether it is the black magic of pagan priests and demon-worshiping aboriginals or the white magic subtly parading under the banner of Christianity. All magic, whether white or black, has its source in the powers of darkness and must be rejected by all believers who would honor the Word of God.

THE PERIL OF BLURRING DISTINCTIONS

But we live in an age when doctrine is being downgraded and experience exalted. Superficially many are seeking in religious experience what drugs, alcohol, or sex can give them in physical experience. They want a thrill, some sensational feeling. They want to be "turned on" religiously.

Not always do they pause to see whether they have the sure direction of the Word of God. Often they do not stop to realize that unless they are "turned on" under the direction of sound Bible doctrine it may turn out that they are "turned on" by demonic dynamic rather than by the Holy Spirit.

Christians must see the true nature of mediumistic powers. It may be said that in pagan lands, where demonized religion has reigned from time immemorial, Christians do. There the overwhelming majority of the people are mediumistically inclined. They readily understand the issues involved.

But in the Western world, where Christianity has had its liberating effects for centuries, the boundaries between the spiritual and the demonic, or mediumistic, are often blurred. Perhaps the main reason for this is that only a tiny minority (compared to the East) are mediumistically inclined. This is increasing with the rising tide of the occult in the decade of the seventies. But it has a long way to go to catch up with the occult-ridden East and primitive pagan cultures in South America and Africa.

On the mission fields of the world, the people who most steadfastly resist the gospel of Christ are those who possess mediumistic abilities. Whenever any of these mediumistic people do come to Christ, however, they at once recognize the true character of their former powers and renounce them as evil and demonic.

This fact contrasts saliently to what often takes place in so-called Christian lands. There the lines of demarcation are fuzzy. Many Christian workers know little or nothing of mediumistic gifts and their clear-cut distinction to the gifts of the Spirit. In fact, many prominent healers and charismatic leaders make a fatal blunder in mistaking these abilities for the genuine gifts of the Spirit. They should renounce them. But how can they do so when they were born and reborn in a context of unsound doctrine that they have never recognized as being such and from which they consequently could never rescue themselves?

Such an unsound doctrinal context, moreover, not only keeps them from detecting the mediumistic nature of certain gifts. Tragically, it encourages them in the cultivation of these mediumistic gifts as instruments of the Holy Spirit. Such abilities should always be renounced. The reason is simple. The Holy Spirit never operates through that which has been won in the realm of occultism or is a carryover or transference from sorcery and witchcraft (cf. 1 Corinthians 10:20-21; 2 Corinthians 6:14-18).

Mediumistic powers always act as a detriment to the spiritual life and service of a child of God. Mediumistic healers and charismatic leaders always leave a trail of division, dissension, spiritual instability, and immaturity in their wake. They do not minister to the unity and purity of the church as the *one* glorious Body of Christ. Nor can they accurately preach the grace of God and salvation by faith alone. Hence, they cannot with assurance and authority present

God's great salvation and the eternal life it brings. Their salvation usually turns out to be man's work, at least in part, rather than totally God's accomplishment. Therefore, it is something that can be forfeited and lost. The life it brings turns out not to be eternal, but life only so long as you merit it by good behavior.

OCCULT RENAISSANCE AND MEDIUMISTIC MANIFESTATIONS

In what is called "a renaissance of the supernatural," the present-day rise of interest in the paranormal and the psychic is giving birth to a whole new brood of mediumistic manifestations in America.[4]

One of the most bizarre is *psychic surgery*. Absolutely incredible to most Americans, this form of mediumistic phenomena is well known in pagan occult-ridden societies in many parts of the world. Spiritists believe that man has an astral body as well as a physical body. Psychic surgeons have ability to perform operations on the astral bodies of people. Without the use of surgical instruments, they merely manipulate their hands above the person's body or actually touch or press it.

The Reverend Harold G. Plume, a psychic surgeon in Monterey, California, claims his powers through the spirit of Hoo Fang, a Chinese physician who lived 2,500 years ago. This alleged spirit (apparently an impersonating demon) appears to Mr. Plume and gives him instructions as to how to perform his psychic operations. Every Sunday these are performed at the minister's church in the presence of his congregation.[5]

In the Philippines, tennis star Tony Roche was relieved of a painful "tennis elbow" by the touch of a psychic healer.[6] People who undergo astral surgery are in some cases undeniably healed of such maladies as gallstones or kidney stones. But usually organic healing is compensated for by very severe psychical complications. In some cases this new problem is more severe than the physical disorder.[7]

Another amazing mediumistic manifestation of the present-day renaissance of the supernatural is *clairvoyance*. This is a paranormal power of persons who, in a trancelike state, are able to discern objects not present to the natural senses and to glimpse future events.

Psychic Jeane Dixon is best known in this area. Besides many incredible predictions, one of her most astonishing prophecies was the Watergate scandal. In the October 21, 1968, edition of the *Washington Daily News* she warned that a wiretapping scandal involving high government officials would erupt during the Nixon administration.

But the famous seeress went a step too far and thereby demonstrated herself to be a psychic clairvoyant and not a true prophetess of the Lord. She stated, "Mr. Nixon, being shocked and appalled at what was perpetrated behind his back, will use his authority to help establish safeguards against the abuse of secret government power."[8]

Psychic Dixon failed the first test that sets apart the true prophet of the Lord from the occult clairvoyant. God's prophets were always 100 percent accurate. "They, in contrast to the frequent misses of the pagan seer, always hit the mark dead center (Deuteronomy 18:20-22)."[9]

Another prominent psychic, who claims even greater accuracy, is Bernadene Villanueva of Tampa, Florida. She interprets the future through colored auras, which she says she sees around people. Red tells of love. Black presages death.

Villanueva catapulated to fame when she envisioned a black aura draping President Kennedy when he visited Tampa, and she predicted his assassination. Two weeks previous to the Nixon resignation, she predicted this event and that Gerald Ford would be in the White House in two weeks.

With such astonishing phenomena as psychic surgery and clairvoyant prognostication taking place in the occult realm, it is high time for alleged miracle healers to examine their doctrines and their methods rigidly in the light of God's Word.

What about clairvoyant abilities to know people and their diseases, without meeting the people? What about people falling "under the power?" Is this the power of God or the psychic power that spiritistic mediums possess? Is this a mediumistic demonstration or the genuine operation of the Holy Spirit unsullied by occult phenomena? The answer is of tremendous import to the seeker of healing and to the believer who wants *only* the will of God and the power of the Spirit.

In every case it may not be easy to decide between the divine and the demonic, but it behooves God's people to go to His Word for guidance. It will be *there*, we may definitely conclude, and *nowhere else* (Isaiah 8:19-20). Such a course is absolutely imperative in a day when there are more than 100 thousand practitioners of white magic in America, not to mention the world.

A back-to-the-Bible approach to the problem is seen to be all the more necessary in the light of the occult subculture in the United States. Already numbering in the millions, the frightening thing is that it is growing rapidly and gives fair promise of mushrooming.

Indeed, this is precisely what the prophetic Scriptures predict for the age-ending era in which we are living. Demonism and false religion will abound (1 Timothy 4:1-2). False prophets will arise (Matthew 24:24; 1 John 4:1-2). Spiritism, witchcraft, and magic are to increase (2 Thessalonians 2:6-7). Diabolical miracles (magic) will deceive many (2 Thessalonians 2:8-10). Satanism will spread with its concomitant moral sag involving violence, sorcery, sexual immorality, and theft (Revelation 9:20-21).

THE BELIEVER AND MEDIUMISTIC MANIFESTATION

Throughout this study it has been shown that in certain instances believers, as well as unbelievers, may possess mediumistic powers. In the case of unbelievers, as we have seen, these may be the result of family inheritance, occult participation, or occult transference. In the case of believers, they normally represent a carryover from the old unregenerate life.

It does seem strange, inasmuch as mediumistic abilities are the result of sins connected with sorcery, that believers should be encumbered with these faculties. In fact, so anomalous does the situation appear that many believers deny that true Christian experience can ever be tainted with mediumistic manifestations. But such a position simply does not face the full implications of God's Word or the obvious facts of human experience.

The problem involved may be illustrated in the salvation of a sinner who has dissipated his youth and his health in debauchery and drunkenness. God's grace abounds where sin abounds. But the man will carry to his grave the scars of his lawless living, and even his children will suffer its effects in various ways.

So it is with people who are saved out of sorcery. In some cases the conversion experience seems to take away all the effects of sin, and any inherited mediumistic powers vanish forever. However, in other cases where the conversion experience is just as real, mediumistic abilities remain, at least in part. These may be unknown to the believer and will remain so, to be discovered later on in the Christian life.

Sometimes these powers are mistaken for the operation of the indwelling Spirit, as we have noted. This can be a tragic mistake. The believer should never use mediumistic abilities in God's service. They should be recognized for what they are—occult operations demonically originated and empowered. They belong to the witch and the medium, to the pagan clairvoyant and the heathen seer, not to the people of God.

As God's people, we, of course, can freely and joyfully use the gifts with which He has endowed us. Moreover, there is nothing wrong with employing help from the scientific or natural realm. But it cannot be overemphasized that mediumistic powers and endowments must be avoided like a spiritual plague. Such enablements originate from the occult activity of ourselves or our forebears. They must be renounced at all cost, because they violate the first two commandments of God (Exodus 20:1-7). They can only stamp our ministry with the mark of rebellion, hinder the Spirit of God, and bring great damage and bondage to ourselves and those who attend our ministry.

THE BELIEVER AND THE MANIFESTATION OF THE SPIRIT

In warning against the danger of mediumistic manifestations, we must be careful not to veer away from the Word and will of God and the dynamic miracle-working ministry of the Holy Spirit.

Mediumistic gifts, at best, are only cheap and tawdry satanic substitutes for the splendid and almighty working of God's Spirit. We have a God who can still work miracles today. And He does so when it brings the highest glory to Himself and redounds to the greatest good of man.

The Lord who fed the five thousand with a few loaves and fish is the Lord of the twentieth century. But He is not performing that miracle where there is a supermarket stacked with food a stone's throw away and He has given men money out of His bounty to buy that food.

Our God is not a sacred clown, as some present-day religious showmen would seem to make Him. He is not standing by as a magician to perform sensational feats to entertain carnal curiosity seekers and to inflate man's ego with pride.

If we, as His redeemed people, are willing to yield ourselves to Him completely to become broken before Him, then we will become partakers of the miracle-working power of the Holy Spirit. Is not this what our Lord referred to when He declared, "Truly, truly, I say to you, he who believes in Me, the works that I do shall he do also; and greater works than these shall he do; because I go to the Father" (John 14:12; NASB)?

What are the works that Jesus did while He was here upon earth that He declared we would do? He did always *only* those things that were in the Father's will (John 5:30; 6:38; Matthew 26:42). Like Him, we shall do those works that are in the Father's will for us. When it is the Father's will for us to do anything Jesus did, we shall be able to do it through the almighty power of the indwelling Spirit.

Does this mean miracles? Yes, when it is the Father's will. Does this mean healing the sick or even raising the dead? Yes, when this is the Father's will. But how will we know the Father's will? Only by *rigid* adherence to the Word, which reveals His will.

Here is where Christians with mediumistic gifts err. They do not always submit to God's will, *which is always in accord with God's Word.* This realm of insubmission to God's Word and will is the realm of Satan and demons. This is the sphere in which mediumistic gifts operate, never the realm of utter yieldedness to God's Word.

But what are "the greater works" to which Jesus referred when He was predicting the coming of the Spirit to indwell His redeemed people? Was He not referring to the fact that in His incarnate, unglorified state He was confined by time and space? But as a result of His death, resurrection, ascension, and the coming of the Spirit to take His place, the millions who are saved would be enabled to continue "to do and teach" (Acts 1:1) what He merely began to do.

They would constitute the mystical Christ (1 Corinthians 12:12), He in heaven joined to His people on the earth, He through them by means of the Spirit doing the far greater world-engirdling works than He ever could have done had He not gone away and given the Holy Spirit to take His place. Thus, through the Spirit, He is working in His Body on earth.

This glorious power of the Holy Spirit is for us. To desire it is not to fall into the trap into which occult-contaminated religionists fall, that is, to use the power and the knowledge of God, independent of God and even in opposition to God. This is the essence of all mediumship and all mediumistic powers and abilities that derive from it.

12

DELIVERANCE FROM DEMON POWER

A s noted throughout this book, the powers of darkness try every trick of their trade to keep ensnared and enslaved those they have trapped. This fact is not only true of the unsaved. It is also true of believers. To accomplish their purpose, satanic forces try to discourage God's people from realistically facing the full biblical witness concerning their activity.

Our Lord, by contrast, spoke quite candidly about Satan and demonic powers. The Word of God, the Holy Scriptures, do the same. Certainly every true follower of the Lord must follow suit. Yet, not every disciple is prepared to do so.[1]

Recently I spoke to a sound, Bible-believing group of Christians who regularly have the Word expounded by competent teachers. One of the believers, an able musician and Bible student, was upset at my presentation of the subject of how far Satan and demonic powers can go in the life and experience of a regenerated person. Having serious domestic and family problems, this believer shied away from a realistic consideration of a subject he declared was negative and depressing. Evidently wearied with the spiritual battle, he wanted to hear no more about war with its ravages and casualties. Peace and victory were what he desired to hear.

But this dear child of God overlooked the fact that he was succumbing to one of Satan's deceptions: "Forget me and my maneuvers, and I'll leave you alone!"

You Must Face the Enemy

It is perilous to ignore the adversary. The apostle Paul realized that. "We are not ignorant of his schemes" (2 Corinthians 2:11; NASB), he declared. It is equally hazardous not to stand against the enemy. The apostle realized that fact, too. "Therefore, take up the full armor of God, that you may be able to resist in the evil day, and having done everything, to stand firm. Stand firm therefore" (Ephesians 6:13-14; NASB).

No one can stand firm against the powers of darkness who does not know his position and resources in Christ and the deceptive schemes of the foe he faces. Christ's glorious salvation and our triumph in Him form the splendid scene that is always brightly silhouetted against the somber background of Satan and demonic activity.

Those who imagine that they can triumph in Christ and not encounter satanic conflict deceive themselves. If they do not experience warfare, either their "triumph" is phony or their position in Christ is purely imaginary. They are parading in the sphere of darkness, but somehow they are mistaking it for the realm of light.

To be delivered from the foe you must know and face the foe. You must claim the efficacy of the blood of Christ and the power of His name. You must face the foe in the light of what you are in Christ and what He has done for you.

Mrs. Gordon C. Timyan, missionary to the Ivory Coast of West Africa, tells the story of a native believer in the mission church who lapsed into demonism. Several years after his conversion, reports circulated that gold had been found in the region. Tempted by an inordinate desire to become rich, he consulted the village fetish man. He was told he would be shown where to find gold if he would give his life over to "a controlling spirit."

This is exactly what this believer did. He made a pact with "the evil one." The demon spirit did enable him to find gold. But the demon exacted a terrible price. The man became so deranged that he could not enjoy his newfound wealth.

Cast out by his family, he became a pitiable spectacle. His dirty body was covered with rags and adorned with various fetish charms. His eyes had a disturbed stare, and his countenance had a wild, distraught look.

Yet, when the church bell rang, he instinctively came to the service. Somewhere in his subconscious mind he knew that he had once found deliverance among God's people and that now his only help was to be found among them.

It was at the church that the missionary couple encountered him. As Mr. Timyan preached one Sunday afternoon, his wife noticed the man's actions. Whenever her husband mentioned the name of Jesus or the Holy Spirit, the man hissed like a serpent while his whole body writhed. When the sermon ended, he scurried away like a frightened animal.

When Mr. Timyan went back to the little church the next Sunday afternoon, the man lingered behind instead of scurrying out after the preaching. Asked if he desired help, he nodded his head while at the same time his body writhed and the serpentlike hissing increased.

The Christians gathered around and prayed. As the missionary prayed, the demon was defeated. The man reeled to the ground, writhed, and hissed. Finally he was quiet. He was delivered that day as he renounced his sin and turned over his redeemed life to God in sincerity. For years he lived a good testimony in the village.[2]

Both the missionary and the believers, as well as the victim, dared to recognize the enemy and face him realistically in the power of their position in Christ. Such recognition of demonic activity with bold confrontation of the powers of darkness is necessary to be set free. Ignorance of Satan's devices and theoretical armchair interpretations of Scripture that simply do not jibe with authenticated human experience hinder rather than help the ministry of deliverance.

Today a new and subtle device of Satan is springing up to distract saints from facing the foe. Because of the flood of anti-occult literature from the evangelical camp that perhaps discloses in some quarters an unhealthy preoccupation with Satan and demonic powers, some believers are falling into another satanic trap. They are loathe to hear anything at all about the powers of darkness. At best, they shy away from facing the full implications of the scriptural teachings on the subject.

This is just as truly a snare of the devil as fanatical occupation with the powers of darkness. If we are going to be delivered, we must face the enemy squarely. We dare not ignore him even if he appears under the masquerade of supposed biblical orthodoxy that sets arbitrary limits to his sway over a sinning saint where such limitations do not really exist.

You Must Trust Christ

But it is futile to face the foe if you do not know and trust the Victor over the foe. Jesus Christ is the Victor. He alone is able to set the captives of Satan free. By His redemptive work on the cross "He delivered us from the domain of darkness, and transferred us to the kingdom of His beloved Son" (Colossians 1:13; NASB). He "disarmed the rulers and authorities . . . made a public display of them, having triumphed over them" through the cross (Colossians 2:15; NASB).

Satan is a powerful foe, but he was decisively defeated at Calvary. If souls shackled by sin and the powers of darkness are unwilling to come to Jesus, there is no hope of deliverance. Believing the gospel and receiving salvation is the starting point of all deliverance. Being taken "out of Adam" and being placed "in Christ" is the *only* ground of rescue (Romans 6:1-11). The lost in Adam can never really be set free.

The gist of the matter is that only through the Son of God, our Savior, can those bound by Satan be set free. "If therefore the Son shall make you free, you shall be free indeed" (John 8:36). Psychiatrists, psychologists, and even theologians are poor substitutes for the Savior, the Redeemer from sin, the Deliverer from the powers of darkness.

A tragic example comes to my mind from my first pastorate years ago. It was during the depression of the 1930s. Temporarily I took a destitute family into the parsonage. The mother and four children all were gloriously saved, but the father never really trusted the Lord as Savior. Try as he would, he could not overcome the evil powers that were deeply entrenched in his life.

Once, when he did not know I was around, I heard demonic voices speaking through him as he fumed and raged in a fit of terrible anger. Eventually this family left the church, but as far as I know this man never was saved and never received deliverance from the evil personalities that had invaded his life and held him captive.

Although our Lord is the sole source of all help, the Spirit of God uses pastors and counselors in the process. These servants of God must themselves be saved and yielded to God's will. They must also be sound in the faith and experienced in leading people to claim the deliverance that is to be found in Christ.

It is also necessary that such counselors have the faith and consequent spiritual authority for their work. They should be able to differentiate between mental illness and what is demonic. Also, they should recognize what cases come in the province of psychiatry or psychology and those that are the result of demonic power.

This is essential so that they may send those cases that are *not* of demon origin to the psychiatrist or psychologist (preferably to one who is a Christian). Such accurate diagnoses will spare many sad mistakes and will enable Christian counselors to deal with cases that really come under their spiritual jurisdiction and to deal with them successfully.

You Must Confess Your Sins

When we trust Christ as our Savior, God forgives *all* our sins—past, present, and future. Never again do we have to face the penalty of them. You say, "What sins then does a saved person have to confess?" The answer is: "The sins he commits daily." These do not affect the believer's standing before God, only his fellowship with God. Confession restores fellowship (1 John 1:9).

If confession is not made and the believer goes on living in sin and broken fellowship, he exposes himself to satanic attack. Blatant, persistent, willful sin gradually exposes him to severe demonization.

To be delivered from demonization, the believer must confess the sins that have brought him to this condition and, through faith, claim the forgiveness and cleansing God promises. This action springing from faith is the first step that disentrenches the powers of darkness. Serious and persistent unconfessed sin gives them the opportunity of digging in and fortifying themselves in the life of the sinning saint.

But demon power in a believer may be the result of a carryover from the old life. This is particularly true of sins of occultism and paganism. People saved out of spiritualism, sorcery, and other types of occultism often find that saving faith in Christ looses them, positionally before God, from all the power of Satan and demons. But this is not always true experientially in their new life.

In fact, many people saved out of demon-ridden idolatry and occultism find that salvation precipitates demonic activity in the new life. The new convert must claim his new position in Christ as the basis for the expulsion of the demons that had power over him before he was saved.

The conversion story of Marina, the wife of a witch doctor in Colombia, South America (in chapter 10), is an example of demonic carryover from a preconversion life that was steeped in spiritism and occultism. The experience of Pat, the Bible student in the Philippines (also in chapter 10), seems to be a combination of a carryover from the old life of occult contamination (his mother was a sorceress) and the sin of wilfulness after he became a believer. The same is true of Vincent, whose deliverance is also recounted in chapter 10.

J. A. MacMillan relates the fearful demon invasion of a true but poorly instructed believer who became deeply involved in spiritism. As a result, this woman, when she came to her senses, realized she had been invaded by the powers of darkness who had intruded and were squatting on God's property.

It took seven whole nights of prayer battle on the part of her pastor and other believers to free this woman of these tormenting spirits. The demons left one by one when ordered to do so by name. But only after the struggle was pushed forward until every demon was defeated was this believer completely set free. The total tally of the ousted demons was almost thirty.[3]

Especially in cases of occult involvement, confession must be specific. Satan hides behind the occult. The power of occult subjection will not be broken unless the specific sin is singled out and confessed: "Father, I confess my sin of consulting a medium, playing with an Ouija board, having my horoscope made, and having my fortune told." Such complicity with occult practice is a direct affront to God and must be brought into the open if deliverance is to be realized.

Often the sin involving occult contamination lies hidden from memory and must be searched out. A young woman at Suwa in the Fiji Islands was troubled with attacks of paralysis. Doctors could find no physical cause whatever. The counselor told her that such trouble often was found in families where spiritism had been practiced. The girl could only remember participating in table-lifting as a youngster. This was undoubtedly the source of her trancelike states of paralysis.[4]

Of course, confession of a demonically enslaved person should not only cover the occult. Every other area of the believer's life should be laid bare before God if experiential victory over satanic forces is to be realized.

You Must Renounce Your Sins

Real confession of sin is inseparable from renunciation of that sin. Confessing without renouncing is failing to face the fact that sin is an affront to our infinitely holy heavenly Father and that it destroys the fellowship of a son in the family (1 John 1:4-9).

But it is hard for a believer in deep sin or under occult bondage to realize the fact that his sins—past, present, and future—have been forgiven and that he simply must believe this. Experienced counselors have found that a barrier seems to lie in the way of the seriously bound saint from believing he is forgiven. Hence, they encourage their counselees to pray a prayer of renunciation.

The prayer of renunciation is of particular importance in cases of the occultly oppressed. Occult activities and sin connected with sorcery are basically of the nature of a contract with the powers of darkness. The contract binds even to the third and fourth generations of occult workers (Exodus 20:5).

Satanic powers continue to claim their rights of ownership. They enforce their claims even upon descendants who are completely unaware of the fact of hereditary complicity and who often have had no contact with sorcery themselves.

However, when a person in this situation is saved, Satan loses no time in trying to enforce his claim. A prayer of renunciation cancels Satan's right officially and judicially. The counselor and other Christians who are present act as witnesses of this annulment of ownership.

In cases of light occult oppression, little difficulty is experienced in repeating the prayer of renunciation. It is only in more serious cases of demonization that trouble occurs. In such instances the demonic power may attack. The victim may easily fall into a trance (the demonized state), and he may cry out in distress that he cannot utter the prayer or say the name of Jesus.

In such cases a protracted prayer battle must be waged to gain deliverance. Recruits in the form of prayer warriors must be called in to assist. When the demonic powers are deeply lodged in their victim, the struggle may be long and intense. But victory is assured because the afflicted person now belongs to Jesus, and the intruders are squatters and can be ousted. They are invaders who have been defeated and need to be hunted down and expelled.

The son of a bishop in Switzerland came to a competent Christian counselor. He was under severe occult bondage. When he tried to pray the prayer of renunciation, his jaws locked and his tongue was paralyzed. All he could do was grind his teeth horribly. This was a case of severe demonization that called for a prayer battle.

The prayer of renunciation finds expression in 2 Corinthians 4:2: "We have renounced the hidden things." When it is prayed, marvelous deliverances occur. In pagan lands where nationals are saved out of a degenerated heathen background, the prayer of renunciation is of great significance. Peter Jamieson, the aboriginal chief of the Wongai tribe, underscored this when he declared, "Many converts backslide through not having renounced before God the various magical practices of their tribe."[5]

You Must Experience Actual Liberation

Loosing a believer from the powers of darkness is sometimes fairly easy, but sometimes it is extremely difficult. The main factor involved is the degree of demonization, which is conditioned by the number of demons with which one is dealing, their wickedness, and the extent to which they are controlling the life.

Our Lord Himself emphasized that some demons are expelled only as the result of a protracted spiritual battle. When the disciples inquired why they were not able to cast the demon out of the epileptic boy, He said to them, "This kind cannot come by anything but prayer" (Mark 9:29; NASB). Many manuscripts add "and fasting," suggesting that the prayer must be effective, intense, and prevailing.

Fasting as an aid to efficacious praying is encouraged in Scripture. Daniel fasted and prayed. On one occasion he did so for a period of three weeks (Daniel 9:3; 10:3). Sometimes much deadly-in-earnest intercession over an extended period is necessary for the expulsion of the demons.

The importance of proper counseling and the power of group prayer cannot be overemphasized in the ministry of actual liberation. In fact, the counselor is only one member of a larger team of prayer warriors. All members of the team must work together if real deliverance is to be achieved (cf. Matthew 18:19; Acts 4:31; 12:12).

The important thing to remember is that the counselor or spiritual diagnostician, determining that the case in question is of a demonic nature, gives the signal for battle. From that point on it is the responsibility of the prayer group that is called in to help join the battle and carry on the struggle *until full victory is won*. This means the contest must not be discontinued *before* complete liberation from demon power is achieved.

People saved out of occultism are frequently still vulnerable to demonic attack, even after actual deliverance. Not only must they learn how to prevail over demonic attacks themselves, but they also need the help of a group of praying believers who will assume the duty of caring and praying for them.

I have counseled with a number of truly born-again people who were saved out of an occult background. Some were troubled with inner voices called *poltergeist* or "noisy spirits." Others were plagued with fearful dreams or nightmarish ghostly appearances.

All of these tormented souls need to recognize the attack of the enemy and learn to claim victory through Christ over him. Meanwhile, they would do well to seek out the help of a prayer group that would undertake to intercede for them before God for their full deliverance, as did Vincent, whose persistent quest for help was rewarded.

An example of how important the support of a band of praying believers is to full liberation from demon power comes from Cordoba, Argentina, where a sick woman visited a spiritist medium. Not only was she healed, but she was amazed to find that the medium had such pronounced mediumistic powers that they were evidently transferred to her, or perhaps her own latent talents were stirred up. Whatever the explanation, this woman found that she could heal others. In fact, she began practicing her newfound art and earned quite a lot of money doing so.

Hearing of this, a Christian medical doctor who was thoroughly conversant of the perils of spiritism, called on the woman. He explained to her what damaging effects the powers of darkness could have on one's life. The woman, deeply impressed by what the doctor said, soon trusted the Lord as her Savior.

But this was the signal for the evil spirits, to whom she had exposed herself by her complicity with occultism, to seek revenge. At night her bed was mysteriously shaken and moved about. Grotesque specters appeared before her eyes. She even saw frogs jumping out of her mouth.

The Christian doctor who had counseled her and led her to trust Christ, realizing the tremendous conflict she was facing, asked a few believers to form a prayer group to intercede regularly for the afflicted woman. As a result, the woman was delivered. Today she is a useful, happy dedicated servant, of the Lord. Prevailing prayer accomplished much in her struggle for victory over unseen spiritual foes.[6]

You Must Destroy Every Occult Object

Idols must be smashed. Fetishes and cult objects must be thrown away. Books of magic must be burned. There must be a clean break with idolatry. People who are unwilling to forsake their occult books and objects need expect no liberation from the powers of darkness.

The revival at Ephesus under Paul's ministry offers an excellent illustration. "God was performing extraordinary miracles . . . so that handkerchiefs or aprons were even carried from his [Paul's] body to the sick, and the diseases left them and the evil spirits went out" (Acts 19:11-12; NASB).

"Many also of those who had believed kept coming, confessing and disclosing their practices. And many of those who practiced magic brought their books together and began burning them in the sight of all; and they counted up the price of them and found it fifty thousand pieces of silver" (Acts 19:18-19; NASB).

Evidently a piece of silver refers to the Greek drachma, which approximated a day's wage (Luke 15:8). The sum, indeed large for those days, illustrates the power of God to deliver men from evil when a clean-cut separation from sin is made.

Real revival in pagan lands always witnesses the destruction of fetishes and objects associated with demon worship and religion. A hidden ban hovers over all magical books. People unwilling to break with this ban never experience deliverance from the dark powers of the spirit world.

J. Merrill Dickinson, a missionary to East Africa, tells the story of the liberation of a witch doctor in a remote area of the field noted for its worship of Satan and the prevalance of demonization. Because of poor roads, the missionary had difficulty getting to the village site where he had been invited by the national African pastor. Leaving his car some distance from the place of meeting, he was met by some national Christians and many heathen. Services were held on Friday and Saturday.

Sunday morning, after the missionary had returned from a prayer service, a witch doctor and two women appeared at the door of the reed house in which he was staying. Immediately the missionary recognized the witch doctor by the symbol of his craft—the wildebeest tail. He was decked with his spears, axes, charms, beads, and herbs. He greeted Mr. Dickinson with the words, "I've come to find salvation. I want deliverance."

Realizing that he faced a real spiritual battle, the missionary sent for all the pastors and their wives. When they arrived, they all talked to the witch doctor, telling him about Christ's redemption and that if he trusted Christ, he must break with all his occult paraphernalia.

He informed the group that he was prepared to do this. The Christians built a fire and burned all the witch doctor's equipment. Then they sang hymns, read Scripture, prayed, and called on God to liberate the man from the devil's grip by Christ's power. As the praying proceeded, the man and the two women gradually removed the charms and beads from their bodies and cast them into the fire.

After several hours of prayer battle, calling on the name of Jesus for their deliverance and claiming the blood of Christ, the witch doctor cried out, "They're going! They are leaving me!"

Meanwhile, however, his leg was being drawn into a knot. But he was gloriously changed, even though he was left a cripple. He gave glowing testimony to Jesus' saving him and delivering him from Satan's grip.

His liberation sparked a revival, and men and women came throughout the day seeking salvation and deliverance. Nine persons were saved and delivered from demonization that day.

Several years later, when the missionary inquired about them, eight had remained steadfastly true. Only one did not make a clean break with occultism and went back into demonism.[7]

You Must Sever Every Mediumistic Contact

To be delivered from occult oppression, a person must sever all relationships with any friends or associates who continue to practice occultism or who persist in any form of demonized religion. The Scripture warning is plain.

> Do not be bound together with unbelievers; for what partnership have righteousness and lawlessness, or what fellowship has light with darkness? Or what harmony has Christ with Belial, or what has a believer in common with an unbeliever? (2 Corinthians 14-15; NASB)

> No, but I say that the things which the Gentiles sacrifice, they sacrifice to demons, and not to God; and I do not want you to become sharers in demons. (1 Corinthians 10:20; NASB)

On the mission field a man who was identified with a group of Satanists was saved and set free from demon bondage. At the time of his salvation he was also healed of a longtime illness. One day this newborn believer visited some of his old friends who were just about to have one of their devil-worshiping meetings. Although the Christian took no part in the ceremonies, he nevertheless remained in the room until the service was concluded. The result was that he exposed himself to satanic attack and his old illness returned.

Never should this believer have been so foolish as to allow himself to associate again with these devil-worshipers. He discovered that God does not permit anyone to treat His commands lightly.[8]

Practically no Christian would seriously question the necessity of breaking off relationship with Satan worshipers and occult practitioners who belong to a believer's old, unsaved life. Yet, there are other relationships that must be guarded against just as carefully but that are more complicated and cause problems and disagreement among believers. This is true of blood relationships. Disastrous trouble can arise unless a newborn believer guards himself against relatives who remain unsaved and continue on in the practice of occultism.

For example, what is a son or daughter to do who is saved in a home where either one or both parents are practicing occultists? If the child is not old enough to be on his own, he will of course be compelled to remain closely associated with what he should be separated from. In such a circumstance the child is in for a rough time, through which God's grace alone can see him.

If the offspring is old enough to be on his own, it would undoubtedly be the wise thing to plan to go to school away from home or to take a job that would get him away from the sinister influence that would surround him. If he remained at home and determined to follow the Lord, his life would be turned into a living hell. Besides, he would run the grave risk of backsliding under pressure and coming under occult bondage.

Such observations and advice might shock many people and arouse great disagreement among some. But the sober fact remains that occultism is a dangerously polluting and enslaving reality. One must separate from it or be ensnared by it.

Counselors experienced in dealing with occultly subjected people sometimes give advice to youngsters saved out of families where parents still cultivate occult practices, which is still more shocking. They warn new converts to be careful how they try to help others before they are themselves strong enough in the faith to help themselves.

Experienced counselors are only too well acquainted with the terrible attacks the powers of darkness can launch against young converts saved out of a strong mediumistic environment. For this reason they sometimes warn children from families where spiritism is practiced not to pray (at least not to do so too soon) for their parents who are still active in occultism. So dangerous is the snare of the occult that even children in relationship to their parents need to ponder the warning: "Be saved from this perverse generation!" (Acts 2:40; NASB).

YOU MUST REPUDIATE EVERY VESTIGE OF DEMONIZED RELIGION

There can be no doubt that the greatest inlet to demon power among God's people is through the ever-widening door of false doctrine and mushrooming cults. Solemnly Scripture warns of the latter-day rise of demonized religion. With stark realism the Bible predicts how this alluring substitute for pure biblical Christianity will vie with revealed truth to capture men's hearts and minds in order to enslave them in error under demon power.

"But the Spirit explicitly says that in the latter times some will fall away from the faith, paying attention to deceitful spirits and doctrines of demons, by means of the hypocrisy of liars seared in their own conscience as with a branding iron" (1 Timothy 4:1-2; NASB).

What happens to believers who fall away from "the faith which was once for all delivered to the saints" (Jude 1:3; NASB)? They listen to demon spirits speaking through false teachers. The result is that they take up with "doctrines of demons," that is, teachings originated and propagated by spirits not from God (cf. 1 John 4:1-2). The cult leaders and promoters of these false doctrines are delineated in realistic terms as "liars," so blinded and set in their errors that their conscience is said to be cauterized unto utter insensitivity to the truths of God's Word. One does not have to go far these days to find believers caught in the net of demonized religion, like a struggling insect enmeshed in a spider's web.

Several years ago I was conducting a Bible conference in Pennsylvania on the subject of "Demonism and Latter-Day Cultism." A family appeared for counseling after one of the sessions. Both the father and mother, as well as their daughter, were stirred by the message of deliverance. They desired to be liberated from the bondage they were in. This was especially true of the grown daughter, who was seriously troubled by demonic activity in her life.

Questioning soon revealed the reason for the spiritistic bondage to which this family had fallen prey. They had become deeply involved in Rosicrucianism, a medley of dangerous occult and philosophic beliefs. It was pathetic to see their momentary interest in the things of God and yet the terrible blindness and insensitivity that enveloped them as they tried to reach out and receive the liberating truth of God's Word. It is still more tragic to realize how these people, like millions caught in cults of perverted Christianity, are held in the vise of false religion under the thrall of demonic blindness and deception.

Although most believers readily accept the fact that they must break off relationships with people who go on practicing occultism, some do not see the necessity of renouncing mediumistic influences and contacts that are to be found in certain fanatical and extreme religious groups. The ever-expanding charismatic confusion in the church today represents a clever halo-crowned stratagem of Satan to divide God's people and to bring them under a very subtle, yet real, type of occult bondage.

Confusion that construes the baptism of the Spirit as something in addition to salvation, instead of a vital inseparable constituent of salvation itself, cannot escape demonic energizing. The reason is simple. Such a variation of a second-work-of-grace theology necessarily casts doubt upon the completeness and sufficiency of the first work of grace—salvation itself.

Such a view simply cannot be squared with the one and only true gospel of salvation by grace through faith and faith *alone* (John 3:16; Acts 16:31; Ephesians 2:8-9). It is a variation of the Galatian heresy, which says that some human work must be added to faith for one to be saved or stay saved. It incurs the risk of the divine anathema (Galatians 1:6-9).

But this is not all. Such a view cannot be brought in line with the believer's unchangeable and unforfeitable position in Christ, a truth indelibly emblazoned everywhere upon the pages of the New Testament. It also represents, in fact, a variation of the Colossian heresy, which denies the believer's completeness in Christ.

This position insists that salvation is not enough. There must be something more, something added, to being united to Christ. It denies the magnificent truth that springs from the person and finished work of the Savior. "In Him all the fullness of Deity dwells in bodily form, and *in Him you have been made compelete*" (Colossians 2:9-10; NASB).

Now, we ask, "How can such an extremely serious and damaging teaching escape enjoying special demonic dynamic?" How can it avoid the scriptural castigation of being "doctrines of demons" (1 Timothy 4:1; NASB)? How can subscription to it fail to expose the believer to despoilment from spirits not from God (1 John 4:1-3)?[9]

But this is not all. What shall be said of adding to this error a second error equally serious, if not more so, since it is erected upon the first? This second error holds that speaking supernaturally in a language never learned is the evidence or proof of having received the so-called baptism of the Spirit.

But how can this be so when *all* Christians are so baptized (1 Corinthians 12:13) and all do *not* speak in tongues (1 Corinthians 12:30)? How can it be so, moreover, when the apostolic revelatory gifts—extrabiblical prophecies, tongues, and extrabiblical knowledge (1 Corinthians 13:8-9)—were meant to be temporary until the divine revelation (the Holy Scriptures) were completed and became available for teaching in the churches (1 Corinthians 13:10)?

When this occurred, these temporary revelatory gifts would no longer be needed. Hence, they were to cease gradually. First Corinthians 14 regulates their use in the apostolic period. Then they were very much needed and therefore in use. Today the church hasn't the slightest need of these gifts that involve extrabiblical revelations. Why? Because it has *the completed Bible itself.*[10]

Believers who insist that tongues should be manifested in the church today, to be consistent, should ordain apostles (1 Corinthians 12:28), countenance extrabiblical prophecies and visions, and condone extrabiblical revelations of knowledge (1 Corinthians 13:8). The Mormons and the Irvingites of the nineteenth century did so. Their mediumistic trends and tendencies should be warning enough to twentieth-century charismatic movements of the danger of demonic activity and consequent risk of occult bondage.

On a recent teaching mission to a midwestern Bible college, a Christian educator told me a heartrending story. His son, a Christian, married a believer. However, after their marriage, this young woman became involved in a charismatic group that was extremely fanatical. It was dominated completely by women.

Women in the group divorced their husbands if they could not dominate them. The only married women were those with henpecked spouses. All the others were either divorced or remarried to men they held under their thumbs. The Christian educator's son became a victim of this sect.

His wife not only would not submit to him, but she divorced him in order to fellowship with a group that she was satanically duped into thinking was superspiritual.

The potential danger of failing to follow scriptural teaching on the gifts of the Spirit was impressed upon me as a young Christian and a college student in 1930. My parents and I were attending what was then Scott Street United Brethren Church in Baltimore. During an evangelistic campaign I remember four women, sitting directly in front of me, putting on a tongues-speaking demonstration in one of the services.

Although almost half a century has passed, I can still see these tongues speakers giving vent to strange sounds from their lips. I witnessed the reaction of these women when the pastor, a genuine man of God and an able Bible student, tried to show them the true teaching of the Word on the subject. All three of the tongues speakers became violently angry and resentful. Their insubordinate and unteachable spirit proved to me that the whole demonstration was not from God.

My study of God's Word and experience in the arena of life for almost fifty years have not altered the situation. Today, as never before, God's people need to be warned of the peril that lies in charismatic movements. Now, as never before, they are disturbing the peace, doctrine, purity, and unity of the church of Jesus Christ. In the age of the occult they are gaining momentum and spreading like a prairie fire.

Unless God's people perceive and obey what the Word says about this issue, they will suffer greater damage. Only as the people of God know and believe what the Word teaches and allow it rigidly to test their experience will the prairie fire be stopped.

Those who do not wish the prairie fire to stop either do not know the damage it is doing or do not know what the Word teaches on the matter. It is high time for those who love the Word of God and are loyal to its precepts to lift their voice and declare its plain directives on the tongues question.

YOU MUST STEER CLEAR OF MAGIC

Magic is a manifestation of the power of evil supernaturalism in the realm of the natural. It is called "white" magic when it masquerades under the guise of light and truth as the operation of the Holy Spirit. It is called "black" magic when it discards its guise and owns its real affinity with the powers of darkness. It is obvious, therefore, that all magic, whether white or black, is evil and represents the operation of the power of Satan and demons.

The prophetic Scriptures foretell a terrifying outburst of magic and occultism at the end of the age. This is predicted to take place before the rapture of the church (1 Timothy 4:1-6; 2 Timothy 3:1-8). But this phase is merely preparatory to the shocking demonization of society after the rapture (2 Thessalonians 2:8-10; Revelation 9:1-12, 20-21; 13:11-15). Then "false Christs and false prophets will arise and will show great signs and wonders," as our Lord Himself foretold, "so as to mislead, if possible, even the elect" (Matthew 24:24; NASB).

Already we find ourselves in the incipient stages of this prophesied outburst of demon activity of the last days. The great apostasy of the thirties, forties, and fifties set the stage for the lawless God-is-dead theology and the so-called "new morality" of the sixties. This in turn opened the way for the age of the demon and the era of occultism and magic of the seventies.

If ever God's people need to adhere rigidly to the Holy Scriptures and its warnings against the specious deceptions of occult-contaminated religion, with its lure of magic, it is now. This danger has been seen in present-day movements to revive *all* the apostolic spiritual gifts. It must also be faced in popular healing movements, which are often associated with tongues groups.

In making some observations and sounding some very necessary warnings on this subject, it must first of all be said that there are true cases of divine healing today. God does heal people according to His will, which is always according to His Word. Only then does He bestow "the prayer of faith" that heals the sick (James 5:14-15). He heals sometimes with and sometimes without natural means.

But God's Word plainly declares that it is *not* always God's will to heal. This is true if the sickness is the result of divine chastening for sin (1 Corinthians 11:30-32) or if it is intended to test and refine the afflicted saint to equip him for finer living and serving (2 Corinthians 12:7-9).

For public healers to assume that it is always God's will to heal an obedient saint is perilous. Sometimes it does not happen to be God's will to do so. To command God in such cases to do what it is not His purpose to do is to make God man's slave or lackey and to get solidly on demon ground.

In such cases the demon (a spirit who opposes the Word and will of God) takes over. Under the guise of white magic (employing the Bible, Jesus' name, etc.) the demon effects a cure of a sort. But in contrast to God's healings, which are gracious and free, demonic healings *always* have a high price attached. They open the door for demonic powers to enter to effect mediumistic or magical cures. These involve a principle of compensation.

Physical healing may take place, but the disorder is merely transferred to a psychic, mental, or emotional upset, or spiritual bondage to some cult results. Or the person "healed" falls prey to false doctrine common among public healers. Worst of all is the enslavement of the conscience to some form of spiritual imbalance of life or fanaticism. Such a bill for a so-called "healing" is just too outrageously high for any child of God to pay. Determining the will of God in the matter of healing (cf. 2 Corinthians 12:8-9) is, therefore, a basic criterion for distinguishing divine healing from the demonic variety.

Another basic criterion to determine whether the healing is by the power of the Holy Spirit (miracle) or by demon power (magic) is relating this phenomenon to Christ's atonement. Public faith healers commonly hold to the belief that physical healing, like spiritual healing (the forgiveness of sins) is in the atonement. This popular notion furnishes the shaky foundations of sand upon which they base their boldness in actually commanding healing in Jesus' name.

But it turns out that spiritual healing (not physical healing) is in the atonement, guaranteeing a future glorified body. A simple proof of this is that the great prophecy concerning physical healing (Isaiah 53:4) was *not* fulfilled on the cross. Matthew distinctly tells us it was fulfilled long before Calvary: "And when evening had come, they brought to Him many who were demon-possessed; and He cast out the spirits with a word, and *healed all who were ill* in order that what was spoken through Isaiah the prophet might be fulfilled, saying, HE HIMSELF TOOK OUR INFIRMITIES, AND CARRIED AWAY OUR DISEASES" (Matthew 8:16-17; NASB).

The great prophecy that our Lord would bear our physical sicknesses and infirmities, accordingly, was fulfilled in His miracle-working ministry. The mighty healings He performed attested Him as the eternal Son of God, the Word made flesh, the divine-human Redeemer, the Savior of the world, the mighty Healer from the disease of sin.

The accomplishment of redemption by our Savior is far grander and more far-reaching than any physical healing effected today, which of necessity will be temporary at best. Spiritual healing assures us of a future glorified, sinless, painless, sickless, deathless body like the Savior's own glorified resurrected body.

Meanwhile, if it is consonant with His all-wise and gracious will to heal us physically, such a blessing of course springs out of His atoning work as Savior, as all spiritual blessings for a fallen race of sinners do. But the blessing itself is not in the atonement as an immediate benefit, as is the forgiveness of sin.

If believers are to escape the snare of magic subtly operating in demonized religion in these last days of increasing demonic deception, they must go to the Word of God. Otherwise they will be exploited in demonized religion by the powers of darkness.

Isaiah's warning was never more desperately needed than now. "To the law and to the testimony: if they speak not according to this word, it is because there is no light in them" (Isaiah 8:20).

You Must Yield Yourself Wholly to God

Yielding one's redeemed life to God is important for joy and victory in the life of every believer. Such presentation of the body as a "living sacrifice" to God, however, is of particular significance to the person saved out of a background of occultism (Romans 12:1-2).

Only as a believer completely yields himself to God can he be filled with the Spirit. Moreover, the powers of darkness are powerless to harm such a believer. When the house is "empty," the demonic powers who have left may return (Matthew 12:43-45).

The case of Pat, the Filipino Bible student, offers a vivid example. Pat represented a very severe case of demonization. As believers dealt with him, they asked the voices coming from him, "In the name of the Lord Jesus, tell us why you are tormenting Pat."

The reply from the demon powers came clearly: "Because he did not surrender his life completely."[1] There was more to the trouble than this, of course, but areas in the redeemed life not yielded to God offer open doors to demon powers. They are eager to seize the slightest opportunity to enter the life of those who were once abjectly enslaved to them. For this reason, a person set free from occult bondage must make a clean sweep of any complicity with evil. It is of extreme importance that he withhold nothing in his life from the Lord.

It might also be added that Christian ministers and counselors who work with the occultly subjected must also at all times maintain a life of complete yieldedness to God. Magicians and sorcerers often attempt to cast spells or do harm to those who under God carry on a ministry of deliverance.

At no time do Christ's servants dare let down the bars. If they do, they run the grave risk of being attacked by the enemy. Those who conduct a ministry of deliverance must themselves be delivered and remain delivered.

Only he who himself is free can be used by God as an instrument of setting others free. He who is free, on the other hand, must be totally God's servant, utterly yielded to Him at all times.

NOTES

Chapter 1

1. Cf. William W. Orr, *The Mystery of Satan*, p. 1.
2. Dave Breese, *His Infernal Majesty*, pp. 1-188.

Chapter 2

1. Stan Baldwin, *Games Satan Plays*, p. 2.
2. Lewis Sperry Chafer, *Satan*, p. 78.
3. Baldwin, p. 4.
4. Cf. Lewis Sperry Chafer, *Major Bible Themes*, p. 124.
5. For Satan's desire to be worshiped, see C. S. Lovett, *Dealing with the Devil*, p.65.
6. John L. Nevius, *Demon Possession*, pp. 41-83.
7. Kurt Koch and Alfred Lechler, *Occult Bondage and Deliverance*, pp. 133-90.
8. Allen Spraggett, *The Bishop Pike Story*, pp. 107-61. For a full account, see Merrill F. Unger, *The Mystery of Bisiop Pike*, pp. 1-114.
9. Cf. Hans Holzer, *The Psychic World of Bishop Pike*, pp. 89-128.
10. Diane Kennedy Pike, *The Search*, pp. 1-137.
11. Ibid., p. 23.
12. Victor H. Ernest, *I Talked with Spirits*, p. 16.
13. For a scriptural evaluation, see James Bjornstad, *Twentieth Century Prophecy —Jeane Dixon, Edgar Cayce*, pp. 13-151. Cf. Sybil Leek, *The Diary of a Witch*, pp. 9-16.

Chapter 3

1. Lewis Sperry Chafer, *Systematic Theology*, 3:273.
2. Ibid.
3. Ibid.
4. William F. Arndt and F. Wilbur Gingrich, *A Greek-English Lexicon of the New Testament*, p. 496.
5. See discussion of "Security" in Merrill F. Unger, *Unger's Guide to the Bible*, pp. 38-39.
6. Lewis Sperry Chafer, *Major Bible Themes*, rev. John F. Walvoord, pp. 224-28.
7. Cf. Lewis Sperry Chafer's classic work, *Grace*, pp. 23-54.

8. Chafer, *Major Bible Themes*, p. 227.
9. Ibid., p. 228.
10. Merrill F. Unger, *The Baptism and Gifts of the Spirit*, p. 19.

Chapter 4

1. Cf. John P. Newport, *Demons, Demons, Demons*, pp. 70-74; and Kurt Koch, *Revival Fires in Canada*, pp. 76-80.
2. Ibid., pp. 74-86; Lewis Sperry Chafer, *Major Bible Times*, rev. John F Walvoord, pp. 158-59.
3. J. A. MacMillan, *Modern Demon Possession*, pp. 18-19; Newport, p. 87; Kurt Koch and Alfred Lechler, *Occult Bondage and Deliverance*, pp. 190-91.
4. Cf. Merrill F. Unger, *Demons in the World Today*, pp. 147-73.
5. *Webster's Seventh New Collegiate Dictionary*, p. 849.

Chapter 5

1. Merrill F. Unger, *Biblical Demonology*, p. 100; cf. J. Stafford Wright, *Christianity and the Occult*, pp. 108-9.
2. Merrill F. Unger, *Demons in the World Today*, pp. 116-17; Kurt Koch, *Christian Counseling and Occultism*, pp. 1-162.
3. Marion Nelson, *Why Christians Crack Up*, p. 145.
4. For a full account, see Frances D. Manuel, *Though an Host Should Encamp*, pp. 39-105.
5. Ibid., p. 44.

Chapter 6

1. Cf. note on Matthew 10:48, *The New Scofield Reference Bible*.
2. Kurt Koch and Alfred Lechler, *Occult Bondage and Deliverance*, p. 69.
3. Ernest Rockstad, *Demon Activity and the Christian*, p. 10.

Chapter 8

1. Plato *Cratylus* I. 398.
2. Joseph Henry Thayer, *A Greek-English Lexicon of the New Testament*, p. 123.
3. See Nicolas Pileggi, "Occult," *McCall's*, March 1970, pp. 61-65.
4. Cf. F. C. Conybeare, "Christian Demonology," *Jewish Quarterly Review* 9 (1896-97): 600-602.
5. For an example, see Kurt Koch, *Demonology Past and Present*, pp. 141-46.

Chapter 9

1. F. F. Bruce, *Commentary on the Book of Acts*, p. 114.
2. For a discussion of Balaam, see Merrill F. Unger, *Biblical Demonology*, pp. 124-27.
3. See chapter 7.
4. See chapter 7.
5. Comment on 1 Kings 22:6 in Charles F. Pfeiffer and Everett F. Harrison, eds., *The Wycliffe Bible Commentary.*
6. Comment on 1 Kings 22:6 in D. Guthrie et al, *The New Bible Commentary.*

Chapter 10

1. See chapter 7.
2. *Webster's Seventh New Collegiate Dictionary*, p. 190.
3. John L. Nevius, *Demon Possession*, p. 190.
4. Ibid., pp. 190-91.
5. Kurt Koch, *Demonology Past and Present*, p. 138.
6. Cf. Kent Philpott, *A Manual of Demonology and the Occult*, p. 120; John P. Newport, *Demons, Demons, Demons*, p. 75.
7. See the amazing case of Mr. Kwo in J. Nevius, *Demon Possession*, pp. 22-29.
8. Koch, *Demonology Past and Present*, pp. 141-47.
9. Oscar W. Jacobson et al, *Attack from the Spirit World—A Compilation*, p. 126.
10. Ibid., pp. 85-87.
11. Ibid., pp. 107-16.
12. Published by Zondervan; see Bibliography.

Chapter 11

1. *Webster's Seventh New Collegiate Dictionary*, Springfieid, Mass.: Merriam, 1971, p. 526.
2. Kurt Koch, *Demonology Past and Present*, p. 61.
3. Cf. Paul Bauer, *Wizards That Peep and Mutter*, p. 83; Kurt Koch, *Between Christ and Satan*, pp. 143-95.
4. Michael Tennesen, "Does the Medium Have the Message?" *Mainliner*, November 1974, p.25.
5. Ibid., p. 27.
6. Ibid.
7. Koch and Lechler, *Occult Bondage and Deliverance*, p. 43.
8. Tennesen, p. 25.
9. Merrill F. Unger, *Beyond the Crystal Ball*, p. 9.

Chapter 12

1. Roger C. Palms, *The Christian and the Occult*, p. 115.
2. Oscar W. Jacobson et al., *Attack from the Spirit World—A Compilation*, pp. 89-91.
3. J. A. MacMillan, *Modern Demon Possession*, pp. 3-5.
4. Kurt Koch and Alfred Lechler, *Occult bondage and Deliverance*, pp. 98-99.
5. Ibid., p. 102.
6. Koch and Lechler, p. 107.
7. Jacobson et al., pp. 197-99.
8. Kurt Koch, *Demonology Past and Present*, p. 152.
9. For a full discussion of the biblical teaching on the baptism of the Spirit, see Merrill F. Unger, *The Baptism and Gifts of the Spirit*, pp. 7-172.
10. For a full discussion, see Merrill F. Unger, *The New Testament Teaching on Tongues*, pp. 1-168; cf. W. A. Criswell, *The Holy Spirit in Today's World*, pp. 167-81.
11. Koch, pp. 141-42.

BIBLIOGRAPHY

Amstutz, Wendell. *Exposing and Confronting Satanism.* Wheaton: Youth for Christ, 1990.

Anderson, Neil. *The Bondage Breaker.* Eugene, Oreg.: Harvest House, 1990.

_____. *Victory Over the Darkness.* Ventura, Calif.: Regal, 1990.

Arndt, W. A., and F. Wilbur Gingrich. *A Greek-English Lexicon of the New Testament.* Chicago: Univ. of Chicago, 1957.

Baker, Roger. *Binding the Devil.* New York: Hawthorne, 1975.

Baldwin, Stan. *Games Satan Plays.* Wheaton, Ill.: Victor, 1971.

Barnhouse, Donald Grey. *The Invisible War.* Grand Rapids: Zondervan, 1965.

Barrett, Ethel. *The Great Conflict.* Glendale, Calif.: Regal, 1969.

Basham, Don. *Can a Christian Have a Demon?* Monroeville, Pa.: Banner, 1972.

_____. *Deliver Us from Evil.* Washington Depot, Conn.: Chosen, 1972.

Bauer, Paul. *Wizards That Peep and Mutter.* Westwood, N.J.: Revell, 1967.

Benner, David G., ed. *Baker's Encyclopedia of Psychology.* Grand Rapids: Baker, 1985.

Bilheimer, Paul. *Destined to Overcome.* Ft. Washington, Pa.: Christian Literature Crusade, 1982.

Bjornstad, James. *Twentieth Century Prophecy—Jeane Dixon, Edgar Cayce.* Minneapolis: Bethany Fellowship, 1969.

Bounds, Edward M. *Satan.* Reprint. Grand Rapids: Baker, 1963.

Breese, Dave. *His Infernal Majesty.* Chicago: Moody, 1974.

_____. *The Marks of a Cult.* Wheaton, Ill.: Christian Destiny, 1973.

Bruce, F. F. *Commentary on the Book of Acts.* The New International Commentary on the New Testament. Grand Rapids: Eerdmans, 1954.

Bubeck, Mark I. *The Adversary.* Chicago: Moody, 1975.

―――――. *Overcoming the Adversary.* Chicago: Moody, 1984.

Burdick, Donald E. *Tongues: To Speak or Not to Speak.* Chicago: Moody, 1969.

Cerullo, Morris. *The Backside of Satan.* Carol Stream, Ill.: Creation House, 1972.

Chafer, Lewis Sperry. *Grace.* Chicago: B.I.C.A., 1939.

―――――. *Major Bible Themes.* Revised by John F. Walvoord. Grand Rapids: Zondervan, 1974.

―――――. *Satan.* Chicago: Moody, 1919.

―――――. *Systematic Theology.* 7 vols. Dallas: Dallas Theological Seminary, 1948.

Criswell, W. A. *The Holy Spirit in Today's World.* Grand Rapids: Zondervan, 1968.

Cruz, Nicky. *Satan on the Loose.* New York: New American Library, 1974.

Dawson, John. *Taking our Cities for God: How to Break Spiritual Strongholds.* Lake Mary, Fla.: Creation House, 1989.

Demon Experiences in Many Lands. Chicago: Moody, 1960.

Dickason, C. Fred. *Angels, Elect and Evil.* Chicago: Moody, 1975.

―――――. *Demon Possession and the Christian.* Westchester, Ill.: Good News, 1989.

Dobbins, Richard. *Can a Christian Be Demon-Possessed?* Akron, Ohio: Emerge, 1973.

Ensign, Grayson H., and Edward Howe. *Bothered? Bewildered? Bewitched? Your Guide to Practical, Supernatural Healing.* Cincinnati: Recovery, 1984.

Ernest, Victor H. *I Talked with Spirits.* Wheaton, Ill.: Tyndale, 1970.

Freeman, Hobart E. *Angels of Light?* Plainfield, N. J.: Logos, 1969.

Gaebelein, A. C. *The Conflict of the Ages.* New York: Our Hope, 1933.

Gasson, Raphael. *The Challenging Counterfeit.* Plainfield, N.J.: Logos, 1966.

Gillesc, John Patrick, *Begone Satan.* Huntington, Ind.: *Our Sunday Visitor*, 1973.

Graham, Billy. *Angels: God's Secret Agents.* Garden City, N.Y.: Doubleday, 1975.

Grant, Jim. *The Enemy.* Wheaton, Ill.: Tyndale, 1973.

Groothuis, Douglas. *Confronting the New Age*. Downers Grove, Ill.: InterVarsity, 1988.

————. *Unmasking the New Age*. Downers Grove, Ill.: InterVarsity, 1986.

Guthrie, D. et al. *The New Bible Commentary*. Rev. ed. Grand Rapids: Eerdmans, 1970.

Hammond, Frank, and Ida Mae Hammond. *Pigs in the Parlor: A Practical Guide to Deliverance*. Kirkwood, Mo.: Impact, 1973.

Hitt, Russell. *Demons Today*. Philadelphia: Evangelical Foundation, 1969.

Holzer, Hans. *The Psychic World of Bishop Pike*. New York: Crown, 1970.

Jacobson, Oscar W. et al. *Attack from the Spirit World—A Compilation*. Wheaton, Ill.: Tyndale, 1973.

Johnson, Jerry. *The Edge of Evil*. Dallas: Word, 1989.

Kallas, James. *Jesus and the Power of Satan*. Philadelphia: Westminister, 1968.

Koch, Kurt. *Between Christ and Satan*. Grand Rapids: Kregel, 1961.

————. *Christian Counseling and Occultism*. Grand Rapids: Kregel, 1965.

————. *Demonology Past and Present*. Grand Rapids: Kregel, 1973.

————. *The Devil's Alphabet*. Grand Rapids: Kregel, 1969.

————. *Revival Fires in Canada*. Grand Rapids: Kregel, n.d.

————. *Satan's Devices*. Grand Rapids: Kregel, 1978.

————. *The Strife of Tongues*. Grand Rapids: Kregel, n.d.

Koch, Kurt, and Lechler, Alfred. *Occult Bondage and Deliverance*. Grand Rapids: Kregel, n.d.

Leek, Sybil. *The Diary of a Witch*. New York: Signet, 1969.

Lewis, C. S. *The Screwtape Letters*. New York: Macmillan, 1956.

Linsey, Hal. *Satan Is Alive and Well on Planet Earth*. Grand Rapids: Zondervan, 1972.

Little, Gilbert. *Nervous Christians*. Lincoln, Neb.: Back to the Bible, 1956.

Lovett, C. S. *Dealing with the Devil*. Baldwin Park, Calif.: Personal Christianity, 1967.

————. *Modern Demon Possession*. Harrisburg, Pa.: Christian Publ., n.d.

MacMillan, John. *The Authority of the Believer*. Harrisburg, Pa.: Christian Publ., 1980.

Manuel, Frances D. *Though an Host Should Encamp*. 5th printing. Fort Washington, Pa.: Christian Literature Crusade, 1973.

Matthews, Victor. *Growth in Grace.* Grand Rapids: Zondervan, 1971.

McLeod, W. L. *Demonism Among Evangelicals and the Way to Victory.* Saskatoon, Sask.: Western Tract Mission, 1975.

Meade, Russell. *Victory over Demonism Today.* Chicago: Christian Life, 1962.

Michaelson, Johanna. *The Beautiful Side of Evil.* Eugene, Ore.: Harvest House, 1982.

Montgomery, John Warwick. *Demon Possession.* Minneapolis: Bethany Fellowship, 1973.

————. *Principalities and Powers: The World of the Occult.* Revised edition. Minneapolis: Bethany Fellowship, 1975.

Montgomery, Ruth. *A Gift of Prophecy—The Phenomenal Jeane Dixon.* New York: Bantam, 1965.

Murrell, Conrad. *Practical Demonology.* Pineville, La.: Saber, n.d.

Needham, Mrs. George C. *Angels and Demons.* Chicago: Moody, n.d.

Nelson, Marion. *Why Christians Crack Up.* Chicago: Moody, n.d.

Nevius, John L. *Demon Possession.* Reprint. Grand Rapids: Kregel, 1968.

Newport, John P. *Demons, Demons, Demons.* Nashville: Broadman, 1972.

Oates, Wayne E. *Religious Factors in Mental Illness.* New York: Association, 1955.

Orr, William W. *The Mystery of Satan.* Wheaton, Ill.: Victor, 1966.

Palms, Roger C. *The Christian and the Occult.* Valley Forge, Pa.: Judson, 1972.

Penn-Lewis, Jesse, and Evan Roberts. *War on the Saints.* Abridged edition. Edited by J. C. Metcalf. Ft. Washington, Pa.: Christian Literature Crusade, 1977.

Pentecost, Dwight. *Your Adversary, the Devil.* Grand Rapids: Zondervan, 1970.

Peterson, Robert. *Are Demons for Real?* Chicago: Moody, 1972.

Pfeiffer, Charles F., and Harrison, Everett F., eds. *The Wycliffe Bible Commentary.* Chicago: Moody, 1962.

Phillips, McCandlish. *The Spirit World of the Bible, the Supernatural, and the Jews.* Wheaton, Ill.: Victor, 1972.

Philpott, Kent. *A Manual of Demonology and the Occult.* Grand Rapids: Zondervan, 1973.

Pike, Diane Kennedy. *Search.* New York: Doubleday 1970.

Pike, James A., and Kennedy, Diane. *The Other Side.* New York: Dell, 1969.

Rockstad, Ernest B. *Demon Activity and the Christian.* Andover, Kas.: Faith and Life, n.d.

Rockstad, Ernest B., and Lulu Jordan Chessman. *From the Snare of the Fowler.* Andover, Kas.: Faith and Life, 1972.

Schneider, Bernard N. *The World of Unseen Spirits.* Winona Lake, Ind.: BMH, 1975.

Scofield, C. I., ed. *The New Scofield Reference Bible.* New York: Oxford, 1967.

Speiser, Ephraim. *Genesis.* The Anchor Bible. New York: Doubleday, 1964.

Spraggett, Allen. *The Bishop Pike Story.* New York: New American Library, 1970.

Tennesen, Michael. "Does the Medium Have the Message?" *Mainliner,* November 1974.

Thayer, Joseph Henry. *A Greek-English Lexicon of the New Testament.* New York: American Book, 1886.

Unger, Merrill F. *The Baptism and Gifts of the Spirit.* Chicago: Moody, 1974.

————. *Beyond the Crystal Ball.* Chicago: Moody, 1973.

————. *Biblical Demonology.* 13th Printing. Wheaton, Ill.: Scripture, 1975.

————. *Demons in the World Today.* 13th printing. Wheaton, Ill.: Tyndale, 1976.

————. *The Mystery of Bishop Pike.* 8th printing. Wheaton, Ill.: Tyndale, 1974.

————. *The New Testament Teaching on Tongues.* Grand Rapids: Kregel, 1971.

————. *Unger's Bible Dictionary.* 26th printing. Chicago: Moody, 1977.

Watson, David. *How to Win the War: Strategies for Spiritual Conflict.* Wheaton, Ill.: Harold Shaw, 1972.

Webster's Seventh New Collegiate Dictionary. Springfield, Mass.: G. & C. Merriam, 1966.

Weldon, John, and James Bjornstad. *Playing with Fire.* Chicago: Moody, 1984.

Weldon, John, and Zola Levitt. *Psychic Healing.* Chicago: Moody, 1982.

White, Thomas B. *The Believer's Guide to Spiritual Warfare.* Ann Arbor: Vine/Servant, 1990.

Whyte, H. A. Maxwell. *Dominion over Demons.* Monroeville, Pa.: Banner, 1973.

Wilburn, Gary A. *The Fortune Sellers.* Glendale, Calif.: Gospel Light, 1974.

Wilson, Clifford, and John Weldon. *Occult Shock and Psychic Forces.* San Diego: Master, 1980.

Wright, J. Stafford. *Christianity and the Occult.* London: Scripture Union, 1971.

Moody Press, a ministry of the Moody Bible Institute,
is designed for education, evangelization, and edification.
If we may assist you in knowing more about Christ
and the Christian life, please write us without obligation:
Moody Press, c/o MLM, Chicago, Illinois, 60610.

235.4
UN57
c.2

9 2003

LINCOLN CHRISTIAN COLLEGE AND SEMINARY

3 4711 00092 8756